P9-DDD-255

Children's Literature: A Very Short Introduction

VERY SHORT INTRODUCTIONS are for anyone wanting a stimulating and accessible way into a new subject. They are written by experts, and have been translated into more than 45 different languages.

The series began in 1995, and now covers a wide variety of topics in every discipline. The VSI library now contains over 500 volumes—a Very Short Introduction to everything from Psychology and Philosophy of Science to American History and Relativity—and continues to grow in every subject area.

Titles in the series include the following:

AFRICAN HISTORY John Parker and
  Richard Rathbone
AGEING Nancy A. Pachana
AGNOSTICISM Robin Le Poidevin
AGRICULTURE Paul Brassley and
  Richard Soffe
ALEXANDER THE GREAT
  Hugh Bowden
ALGEBRA Peter M. Higgins
AMERICAN HISTORY Paul S. Boyer
AMERICAN IMMIGRATION
  David A. Gerber
AMERICAN LEGAL HISTORY
  G. Edward White
AMERICAN POLITICAL
  HISTORY Donald Critchlow
AMERICAN POLITICAL PARTIES
  AND ELECTIONS L. Sandy Maisel
AMERICAN POLITICS
  Richard M. Valelly
THE AMERICAN PRESIDENCY
  Charles O. Jones
AMERICAN SLAVERY
  Heather Andrea Williams
THE AMERICAN WEST Stephen Aron
AMERICAN WOMEN'S HISTORY
  Susan Ware
ANAESTHESIA Aidan O'Donnell
ANARCHISM Colin Ward
ANCIENT EGYPT Ian Shaw
ANCIENT GREECE Paul Cartledge
THE ANCIENT NEAR EAST
  Amanda H. Podany
ANCIENT PHILOSOPHY Julia Annas

ANCIENT WARFARE Harry Sidebottom
ANGLICANISM Mark Chapman
THE ANGLO-SAXON AGE John Blair
ANIMAL BEHAVIOUR
  Tristram D. Wyatt
ANIMAL RIGHTS David DeGrazia
ANXIETY Daniel Freeman and
  Jason Freeman
ARCHAEOLOGY Paul Bahn
ARISTOTLE Jonathan Barnes
ART HISTORY Dana Arnold
ART THEORY Cynthia Freeland
ASTROPHYSICS James Binney
ATHEISM Julian Baggini
THE ATMOSPHERE Paul I. Palmer
AUGUSTINE Henry Chadwick
THE AZTECS David Carrasco
BABYLONIA Trevor Bryce
BACTERIA Sebastian G. B. Amyes
BANKING John Goddard and
  John O. S. Wilson
BARTHES Jonathan Culler
BEAUTY Roger Scruton
THE BIBLE John Riches
BLACK HOLES Katherine Blundell
BLOOD Chris Cooper
THE BODY Chris Shilling
THE BOOK OF MORMON
  Terryl Givens
BORDERS Alexander C. Diener and
  Joshua Hagen
THE BRAIN Michael O'Shea
THE BRICS Andrew F. Cooper
BRITISH POLITICS Anthony Wright

Kimberley Reynolds

CHILDREN'S LITERATURE

A Very Short Introduction

OXFORD
UNIVERSITY PRESS

Great Clarendon Street, Oxford ox2 6DP

Oxford University Press is a department of the University of Oxford.
It furthers the University's objective of excellence in research, scholarship,
and education by publishing worldwide in

Oxford New York

Auckland Cape Town Dar es Salaam Hong Kong Karachi
Kuala Lumpur Madrid Melbourne Mexico City Nairobi
New Delhi Shanghai Taipei Toronto

With offices in

Argentina Austria Brazil Chile Czech Republic France Greece
Guatemala Hungary Italy Japan Poland Portugal Singapore
South Korea Switzerland Thailand Turkey Ukraine Vietnam

Oxford is a registered trade mark of Oxford University Press
in the UK and in certain other countries

Published in the United States
by Oxford University Press Inc., New York

© Kimberley Reynolds 2011

The moral rights of the author have been asserted
Database right Oxford University Press (maker)

First published 2011

All rights reserved. No part of this publication may be reproduced,
stored in a retrieval system, or transmitted, in any form or by any means,
without the prior permission in writing of Oxford University Press,
or as expressly permitted by law, or under terms agreed with the appropriate
reprographics rights organization. Enquiries concerning reproduction
outside the scope of the above should be sent to the Rights Department,
Oxford University Press, at the address above

You must not circulate this book in any other binding or cover
and you must impose the same condition on any acquirer

British Library Cataloguing in Publication Data

Data available

Library of Congress Cataloging in Publication Data

Library of Congress Control Number: 2011934704

Typeset by SPI Publisher Services, Pondicherry, India
Printed in Great Britain
on acid-free paper by
Ashford Colour Press Ltd, Gosport, Hampshire

ISBN 978-0-19-956024-0

10

For my mother and siblings, who share my appreciation of children's books, and in memory of Colette, who introduced me to some of the best of them.

Contents

Acknowledgements

This book is the product of years of teaching and conversations with students and colleagues too numerous to mention individually, though I hope you know who you are. Four must be singled out, however. As always, Peter Hunt, Peter Reynolds, and Nicholas Tucker were my first readers. Your patience and perseverance are appreciated. Hazel Sheeky also read and commented on drafts. The School of English Literature, Language and Linguistics at Newcastle University gave me some leave to write the book, for which I am extremely grateful. My editor at OUP, Andrea Keegan, asked and waited for it. Thank you. Thanks too to Emma Marchant, who ably handled the minutiae.

List of illustrations

Introduction: what is children's literature?

Outside academia, the term 'children's literature' has a largely unproblematic, everyday meaning. From newspapers and other media to schools and in government documents, it is understood to refer to the materials written to be read by children and young people, published by children's publishers, and stocked and shelved in the children's and/or young adult (YA) sections of libraries and bookshops. Occasionally, questions are asked about whether something is suitable for a juvenile audience, a question usually provoked by concern about content – is it too sexually explicit? Too frightening? Too morally ambiguous? Sometimes questions of suitability reflect concerns about style – will grammatically incorrect or colloquial language or writing that includes swearing or abusive language or experimental writing counteract lessons taught in school or instil bad habits? More recently, as large numbers of adults have been reading books that were originally published as children's literature (the *Harry Potter* books, *His Dark Materials*, *The Curious Incident of the Dog in the Night-time*, *The Book Thief*, *Persepolis*), there has been some debate about whether such books are suitable for adults, and if this kind of reading is a symptom of the dumbing down of culture. For the most part, however, what children's literature is, is taken for granted.

For those who research and teach children's literature, by contrast, the term is fraught with complications; indeed, in one of the most controversial studies of children's literature of the last century, Jacqueline Rose (1984) referred to the 'impossibility' of children's literature. Rose was in fact referring to the nature of the adult–child relationship in children's fiction, and her concerns, as well as other of the more theoretical issues that complicate the study of children's literature, are discussed in Chapter 2. But in many ways, even at a practical level, children's literature is 'impossible': impossibly large and amorphous for a field of study. In truth, there is no clearly identifiable body of 'children's literature' any more than there is something that could be called 'adults' literature', nor are the two areas of publishing as separate as these labels suggest. Both reflect ideas about the purpose, nature, and modes of writing at any given moment; they share a technology, a distribution system – often the very producers of works for adults and children, and even some of the texts, are the same. Nevertheless, the term 'children's literature' is widely used, and so before it can be discussed, how it is used needs to be understood.

Currently, everything from folk and fairy tales, myths and legends, ballads and nursery rhymes – many of which date back to preliterate epochs – to such embodiments of our transliterate age as e-books, fan fiction, and computer games may come under the umbrella of children's literature. Additionally, as an area of research and teaching, children's literature encompasses all genres, formats, and media; all periods, movements, and kinds of writing from any part of the world, and often related ephemera and merchandise too. It addresses works that were specifically directed at the young, those that came to be regarded as children's literature by being appropriated by young readers, and those that were once read by children but are now almost exclusively read by scholars. Chapter 2 looks at the consequences of this variety on how children's literature is studied; here it is important to establish that there is no single, coherent, fixed body of work that makes up children's literature, but instead many children's literatures produced at different times in different ways for different purposes by different kinds of people using different formats and media.

Despite its vagaries, there is much consensus about what is studied by those who work in the field, and one purpose of this *Very Short Introduction* is to map out some of the common assumptions about what children's literature is as an area of research and teaching. A sense of the range of material classified as children's literature – and so the impossibility of doing justice to it in the kinds of surveys that typically constitute introductions to this field – can be gained by looking at how histories of the subject are organized, and considering what has been classified as writing for children and how that has changed over time. There are several intrinsic problems with taking a historical approach, not least the fact that it risks implying that there has been a progressive evolution culminating in the understanding and production of children's literature as it exists today. It is difficult to avoid this impression when organizing material chronologically, but the history provided in the first chapter attempts at least to limit such an implication by presenting material in terms of change and continuity rather than progress.

Another point to bear in mind is that until recently, histories of children's literature were almost exclusively produced in and about those Western countries that had strong traditions of publishing for children, and it tended to be scholars, collectors, librarians, and enthusiasts from those countries who organized conferences, launched journals, and developed terminology for discussing texts for children. This legacy has shaped attempts to define children's literature, what has been included in histories of the genre, and how it is valued and approached by scholars, to such an extent that in many countries where children's literature is studied, it is often works from Britain, other parts of Western Europe, and the USA that tend to dominate. This obscures many other traditions and the extent to which Western children's

3

literature has been enriched by stories and characters, writers and illustrators from many parts of the world. Globalization and use of the Internet have further skewed this trend in favour of Anglophone publications, and so, while on one level it grossly misrepresents the history of children's literature, the outline history set out in Chapter 1 is based on works published in English, even if they were first written in another language. In fact, long before the current phase of globalization, as a consequence of migration, colonization, missionary and trade activities, or occupation, there was considerable commonality in what children read in many parts of the world, so this broadly Anglo-American history will have a family resemblance to histories of children's literature in many countries.

The cultural value of children's literature

Because children's literature is one of the earliest ways in which the young encounter stories, it plays a powerful role in shaping how we think about and understand the world. Stories are key sources of the images, vocabularies, attitudes, structures, and explanations we need to contemplate experience; because when directed to children they are often bound up with education of one kind or another, they can be important carriers of information about changes in culture, present and past. Indeed, its long history and the fact that writing for children straddles the domestic and institutional, official and unofficial, high and mass cultures, and often includes visual elements, means that material written for children can be a particularly valuable source of historical information about everything from how children in the past looked and the environments they occupied, to shops, servants, the treatment of disease, religion, wars, migration, scientific development, exploration, and much more.

Children's literature's links to the past work at multiple levels, too. Just as the children we once were continue to exist inside and to affect us, so writing produced for children continues to resonate over time and to be implicated in the way societies are conceived, organized, and managed. This is not a straightforward process; traditional ideas may be preserved in earlier texts, or deliberately promoted in conservative contemporary works or unconsciously perpetuated in those that uncritically hold up a mirror to current social trends. At the same time, many stories given to children today are retellings of traditional stories in which writers and illustrators set out to expose, critique, and adjust the schemata by which we interpret the world. The dialogue they create between old and new ways of thinking can be another way both to sow and to nurture the seeds of social change, as seen in the way children's literature has contributed to developments in the areas of equality and diversity. This capacity was of particular interest to Walter Benjamin, who collected children's books and valued the potential of writing for the young to radicalize rising generations, encouraging them to resist established ways of thinking promoted through formal schooling. Whether radical or conservative, meritorious or meretricious, writing for children is a rich but for long undervalued source of information about culture as well as a contribution to it.

Chapter 1
An outline history of publishing for children in English

Beginnings

Although *Aesop's Fables*, translated and printed by Caxton in 1484, is usually included somewhere in histories of children's literature, until the end of the last century, histories of writing for children tended to begin in the 17th century, with examples of works by religious dissenters, usually starting with the Czech educational reformer John Amos Comenius's *Orbis Sensualium Pictus*. Written in German in 1658, *Orbis Pictus* was available in an English translation the following year in an edition that remained in print until the 19th century, including a re-illustrated version produced in the US in 1810. The history of this small book – it measured just 142 x 83 mm (roughly 6 x 3 inches) – reveals much about the history of writing for children, not least how, long before instant communication and globalization, some children's books rapidly moved between countries. *Orbis Pictus* was translated into many European languages. In all editions, it begins with the alphabet, then, through a combination of words and pictures, seeks to represent everything in the world (orbis), from creatures and plants to abstract concepts such as the Holy Trinity.

Orbis Pictus typifies several aspects of early writing for children, beginning with its assumptions about age. Comenius was writing for very young children; those under six years old who were

1. Comenius's bilingual (Latin + another language) didactic text is also an ambitious picture book that tries to provide an image to represent each noun it names, no matter how abstract. It aims to teach by entertaining children

learning to read in their own language and then, from six, in Latin (the text was bilingual in the local language and Latin). While the youth of the intended reader has been a defining feature of children's literature throughout its history, since Comenius's day, childhood as a period of life has expanded steadily to the extent that some recent works produced by children's publishing houses are for 'young adults' as old as 18. Until the 19th century, however, books for children were directed at those who were prepubescent and often entering or in the early stages of their education. Having learned to read, children for the most part shared texts with adults, whose reading abilities were often at much the same level. For instance, both young and old might read chapbooks – small, inexpensively produced pamphlets which started to appear in the 16th century. With their simple texts (generally based on popular

7

tales, ballads, and similar folk materials) and woodblock illustrations, chapbooks attracted young readers, though it was not until the 18th century that examples specifically for children began to appear.

Orbis Pictus was intended as a teaching tool, and a strong dialogue between educational theories and writing for children runs throughout the history of children's literature, although today it is common to distinguish between information/educational books such as Comenius's and fiction, now the dominant force in children's literature. When tracing the origins of children's literature, however, histories generally include all forms of writing specifically for children, and regard *Orbis Pictus* as a landmark. Like *Orbis Pictus*, during the 17th century much writing for children was inspired by the group of religious dissenters often referred to as Puritans, so, as well as teaching children how to read, it also sought to teach them how to live godly lives, seek grace, and attempt to avoid the torments of hell. A typical example of such writing originating in England is James Janeway's *A Token for Children* (1671/2), which purports to be the eyewitness testimony of '*the Conversion, Holy and Exemplary Lives, and Joyful Deaths of several young Children*', as the subtitle explains.

Janeway's volume, popular both in England and America (in an enlarged edition by Cotton Mather published in 1700) for some 200 years and regularly reprinted as well as expanded and retold, is a useful milestone in any account of the origins and development of children's literature. It clearly addresses young readers (though it also assumes adults will be involved in the reading process, as indicated in the opening letter to parents and all those who are involved in the education of children) and offers a range of insights into how children and childhood were understood in early modern England. With its unashamedly didactic content, teacherly style, and assumption that children are born sinful, *A Token for Children* points to the relationship between constructions of childhood at any given period and the history of writing for children; that relationship has become a key area of interest in the study of children's literature. Puritan texts are also often used to support the view that the history of children's literature is one that moves from the conviction that writing for children should concentrate on instructing its readers on how they ought to behave and what they should believe to the desire to entertain them. Largely uncontested for many decades, this interpretation of the development of children's literature is now regarded as reductive, for many early children's writers understood the need to use 'cobwebs to catch flies', imparting messages inside writing made appealing through the use of child characters, rhymes, puzzles, riddles, dramatic dialogues, and references to children's games. The many new digital resources that make access to pre-1900 texts readily available online make it possible for anyone interested in this debate to sample a wide range of what was published for children before 1900 and ascertain how closely education and entertainment were intertwined.

One reason why the first histories of children's literature often began in the 17th century is because by this time materials for children were being printed for public distribution rather than produced by hand for private use or extracted from writing for adults. This establishes them as part of print culture, and an interest in the history of printed materials was often a starting point for early histories of children's books. Because relatively few items were produced for children, as seen in the cases of Comenius and Janeway, popular works remained in print for long periods, often in a variety of illustrated formats, and frequently feature both in collections and in memoirs. For example, Charles Lamb, born in 1775, recalls loving 'a great *Book of Martyrs*' (*Foxe's Book of Martyrs*, first published in 1554 and translated into English in 1563). Their long and varied histories make such works interesting case studies from multiple perspectives: they can be used to explore printing and marketing techniques, changing ideas about childhood and education, prevailing debates about religion, politics, gender, science, the experience of everyday life, and much more. As interest in the histories of childhood, the book, and children's literature has developed, new materials are also being studied, for it has become clear that writing for children began long before James Janeway and his contemporaries.

Children's literature in antiquity and the Middle Ages

Seth Lerer's (2008) history of children's literature includes a discussion of Greek, Roman, and medieval texts given to the young. Lerer shows that in each of these periods, traditions were established that had an enduring, but for long unacknowledged, influence on children's literature (the materials Lerer discusses were written in Latin, but, as seen in *Orbis Pictus*, Latin was for centuries central to education, so such works influenced texts written and read in English). Greek and Roman children, for instance, were taught the skills of citizenship, the qualities of heroism, the intricacies of morality, and behaviour appropriate to the sexes by learning to recite passages from texts including the fables of Aesop, the *Iliad*, and the *Aeneid*. While what they were learning were passages from existing texts for a general audience rather than those specifically written for children, the way these texts were adjusted to suit the needs and interests of the young brings such works into the domain of children's literature. For example, extracts were chosen as appropriate for children, adapted to suit their abilities, and made to appeal to them by employing elements such as rhyme and including illustrations. During the Middle Ages in Britain and across Europe, these features were employed in writing specifically for children – from the 'mirror for princes' with its lessons for kings, through guidance for apprentices, to advice for children being raised in monasteries and learning the virtues of a devotional life. It is from these, Lerer proposes, that many of the genres that continue to feature in writing for children emerge.

New areas of scholarship bring to light new examples of writing for children, subtly altering longstanding landmarks in the history of children's literature. For instance, traditionally, histories of children's literature celebrated the arrival of commercial publishing for children in the 18th century as the moment when children's literature as we know it today begins. While it remains the case that the potential to sell printed materials of many kinds to children was first exploited by 18th-century printer-publishers, it is now clear that this was not a spontaneous development. Instead, it is part of a literary continuum in which parents, teachers, and other adults involved with the young had for a long time been experimenting with ways of creating attractive and engaging materials for children to read.

The business of publishing for children: 18th-century innovations

A breakthrough in understanding the forces that shaped commercial publishing for children in the 18th century was the discovery in the 1990s of the hand-made materials for teaching her children to read created by Jane Johnson in the 1740s. Johnson's beautifully produced cards, mobiles, toys, and personalized books for and featuring her children provide clear evidence of a tradition of creating children's literature at home, that drew on current educational advice and practice, but tailored it to suit the specific needs of known children. Research following the discovery of Jane Johnson's materials has established that commercial publishers were not inventing *new* ways of writing for children, but adapting practices that had existed in a variety of forms for centuries. It is now apparent that leading figures in the field – printer-publishers such as John Newbery (1713–67), Mary Cooper (d. 1761), John Harris (1756–1846), and William Godwin (1756–1836) – were attempting to reproduce the association between homemade reading materials and a caring adult, usually a mother, reading to and teaching children, with a view to substituting their own printed versions of these materials for

11

This Girl to get money does dance on a Rope.
She will sure have good luck if her neck is not broke
Quite hard is her fortune, her fate most unkind
If no way for a living but this she can find.

2. *This girl to get money*... one of the numerous cards made by Jane Johnson for her children in the 1740s

those made at home. (Presumably, most such homemade items were less carefully made and less well cared for than those in the Johnson family.)

Unlike parents, printer-publishers were producing reading materials for children in order to sell them, meaning their products had to attract and satisfy the adults who purchased the books and other materials they printed as well as – and probably before – child readers. The sense of a combined audience of adults and children is also evident in earlier works, an example being the letter to parents, exhorting them to spare no effort to save their children, with which Janeway begins *A Token for Children*. In the hands of the 18th-century professionals – printers, publishers, picture-makers, and pedagogues – the practice of simultaneously addressing adults and children becomes institutionalized. Perhaps to counter the effects of the address to adults, those involved in producing printed materials for the young began to experiment with paratextual features specifically designed to establish particular works as *for* children. These experiments sometimes focused on size – many books included the word 'little' in their titles, and the books themselves were often very small, as in the case of the ten-volume *The Lilliputian Library* (1779), each volume of which was 99 x 78 mm (4 x 3 inches). Other ways to create juvenile appeal were the use of brightly coloured endpapers, colour, illustrations, cut-outs, and novelty packaging such as sets of books that resemble miniature libraries. These elements made it easy to identify books for children. In doing so they underlined the idea that children should have access to books and so supported sales. Their presentation implied that such items were suitable and good for children.

3. The combination of diminutive size and detailed presentation – book case and library–style shelves full of complete miniature books – is characteristic of the creative energy that went into marketing to juvenile readers

Of course, as ideas about childhood change, understanding of what is suitable for children and what children will enjoy also changes, meaning that to modern eyes, it can be hard to understand the appeal of many of the materials that were popular in their day. However, there is considerable evidence to show that many books from this period, including those such as John Bunyan's *The Pilgrim's Progress* (1678) which were not written for children but repackaged for them, continued to be loved by young readers long after they first appeared. For instance, in 1862, the British writer George Crabbe wrote to a friend that his six-year-old daughter was so caught up in Bunyan's tale that 'The dear child was caught reading by her sleeping maid at five o'clock this morning, impatient, 'tis our nature, to end her pleasure.' Similarly, characters and expressions became so familiar that they entered into common parlance and survive to this day. Newbery's 'Goody Two-Shoes' is an example of the former, while it would be hard to find an anthology of children's verse that did not contain one of the poems first brought together in *Tommy Thumb's Pretty Song Book, Voll.* [sic] *II* (1744), among them 'Bah, bah black sheep', 'Who did kill Cock Robin', 'Boys and Girls Come out to Play', and 'Ladybird, Ladybird'.

What adults deem 'suitable' does not always correspond to what children enjoy or are curious to read, however. Another area of children's literature scholarship that is changing understanding of the history of the subject is the examination of how 18th-century children read and responded to the materials they were given on the evidence of such things as marginalia and graffiti, and how far they were involved in the selection process. Juxtaposing comments and drawings in books once owned by children against images of children with books, or attempting to sneak access to books put out of reach, provides glimpses into how far children may have resented or enjoyed what they were given to read – and desired what they were forbidden to read. This kind of analysis is typical of the way understanding of where children's literature fits into the histories of reading, print culture, and childhood is expanding as more researchers from a variety of backgrounds enter the field.

The commercial, pedagogic, and philosophical forces that shaped publishing for children in the 18th century were set in the context of the Enlightenment, with its commitment to reason, scientific thinking, and progress. As in antiquity, writing for children was considered part of educating them to become valuable citizens; as well as helping them learn to read, then, children's literature warned against superstition and the dangers of failing to acquire a well-rounded education. It taught the principles of reasoning and contemplated such topical injustices as slavery. In general, the implied child readers of 18th-century children's texts were freed from the taint of original sin characteristic of 17th-century writing for children; nevertheless, works for children regularly reminded readers of their ignorance, lack of experience, and fallibility. Stories such as those in Maria Edgeworth's *The Parent's Assistant* (1796) underline the need for constant vigilance and guidance on the part of adults to prevent children falling by the wayside.

Traditionally, historians of children's literature have characterized 18th-century writing as continuing the earlier bias towards instruction, with entertainment only coming to the fore in the hands of such 19th-century writers and illustrators such as Washington Irving (1783–1859), Nathaniel Hawthorne (1804–64), Edward Lear (1812–88), Charles Kingsley (1819–75), Louisa May Alcott (1832–88), Lewis Carroll (1832–98), Walter Crane (1845–1915), Randolph Caldecott (1846–86), Kate Greenaway (1846–1901), Joel Chandler Harris (1848–1908), and Howard Pyle (1853–1911). So much work of high literary and artistic merit appeared in the second half of that century that it came to be known as a 'Golden Age' of children's literature. But such broad-brush labels are increasingly understood as reductive; there was much to amuse and entice earlier readers and a considerable body of badly written, heavily didactic writing for children was published in the 19th century. It is the case, however, that in the course of the 19th century, the rational but ignorant child as figured in Enlightenment children's literature gradually gave way to more complex constructions of children – both as characters and readers – while developments in printing technology made it possible to produce a vast array of colourful, attractively designed books, periodicals, and printed novelties for children in large quantities at a variety of prices.

Children's literature became a highly profitable area for many publishers, not least religious publishing houses such as the Religious Tract Society (RTS, from 1799) and the Society for Promoting Christian Knowledge (SPCK, from 1698), which set out to counteract the kind of popular literature typified by the more sensational end of chapbook publishing and the lurid publications known as 'penny dreadfuls'. While most of these were not written for children, they were often read by them. Publishers like the RTS and SPCK, and the many commercial publishers who followed their example, fought fire with fire by using similar narrative and presentational strategies – vivid plots, empathetic young characters, and bold illustrations – to deliver messages in keeping with the religious bodies they represented. Their respectable motives did not necessarily result in tedious texts; to show the consequences of sin, the plots of such works had first to feature vice and villainy, while to inspire charity, writers told pitiful tales of woeful child victims and virtuous mothers worn to death by the hardships of poverty. By the end of the 19th century, publishing for children spanned everything from these evangelical tearjerkers through fantasy, fairy tales, nonsense, and an array of genres including adventure, animal, and school stories. There were also innovative picture books and periodicals. The business of publishing for children had become so dynamic and commercially successful that in 1899, while contemplating 'The Future of the Novel', Henry James crossly observed:

> The literature, as it may be called for convenience, of children is an
> industry that occupies by itself a very considerable quarter of the
> scene. Great fortunes, if not great reputations, are made we learn,
> by writing for schoolboys....

Much of James's disgruntlement stemmed from the fact that he
was working to produce high-quality, high-status literature, and
felt his efforts were hindered by a marketplace that did not
adequately distinguish between good writing and that enjoyed by
those he regarded as 'irreflective and uncritical', specifically, women
and children. In fact, by the end of the 19th century, the publishing
marketplace was making fine distinctions between readers, and
nowhere more so than in the highly stratified area of publishing for
children, which deliberately divided its audience into categories
and catered for readers of different ages, classes, incomes, interests,
and both sexes. But James had a point: what today is called
'crossover fiction' – texts that appeal to mixed audiences of adults
and children – existed in the past, too. Originally, it was more
common for children to 'cross over' to the domain of adult texts,
taking such works as they found rewarding for their own. Many of
the earliest texts usually included in histories of children's
literature are of this type, with *The Pilgrim's Progress*, *Robinson
Crusoe* (1719), and the novels of Charlotte M. Yonge (perhaps
especially *The Daisy Chain*, 1856) being examples. But just as late
20th-century adults were drawn to the *Harry Potter* books and *His
Dark Materials*, so many books for children during the 19th
century had a large and unapologetic following among adults.
Early examples of crossover fiction included Charles Kingsley's *The
Water-Babies* (1863); both of Lewis Carroll's *Alice* books (1865,
1871); Hesba Stretton's waif story *Jessica's First Prayer* (1867), and
much of Mark Twain's work (1835–1910). Probably the most
significant area of crossover readership was the boy's adventure
story. Presidents and prime ministers were among the many grown
men who credited boys' stories such as those by Captain Mayne
Reid (1818–83) and G. A. Henty (1832–1902) with teaching them

17

about the natural world, history, and geography when they were young, and who as grown-ups were enthusiastic readers of Robert Louis Stevenson's stories for boys, especially *Treasure Island* (1881).

Henry James complained about stories for schoolboys, but an equally well-developed body of writing for girls had also grown up during the 19th century. When commercial publishing for children began, girls and boys generally shared the same books and stories, even if they came with slightly different paratextual trappings. For instance John Newbery's *A Little Pretty Pocket-Book* (1744) was intended 'for the instruction and amusement' of both 'Little Master Tommy' and 'Pretty Miss Polly', and came with a two-toned ball for boys or pincushion for girls into which each was instructed to ask their Nurse to insert a pin on the red side for good actions and the black side for bad. As part of the 19th-century stratification of markets, many books were targeted at boys *or* girls. Often, these were parallel stories – books set in boys' schools and those set in schools for girls, for example – but there were also generic differences: adventure stories tended to be addressed primarily to boys, while domestic and family stories targeted girls. Despite the fact that most girls' stories lacked the exotic settings and exciting plots typical of tales of discovery and battle for boys, many memorable young female characters were created at this time and have continued to attract enthusiastic followers. North American writers were particularly good at creating books with dynamic and engaging girl characters, foremost among them Louisa May Alcott's Jo March (*Little Women*, 1868), but there was a pre-existing tradition of novels about such girls. For instance, Swiss author Johanna Spyri's *Heidi* (1880–1, translated 1884) had a following well into the last century, and in 1937 was one of the first children's books to become a Hollywood film, when it became a vehicle for Shirley Temple. The flow of appealing girl characters from North America continued into the next century with *Anne of Green Gables* (1908), *Rebecca of Sunnybrook Farm* (1903), and *Pollyanna* (1913).

Children's books for a child-centred age

The spate of lively girl characters in the early 1900s is symptomatic of the cultural romance with the idea of childhood (as distinct from real children) that characterized the turn of the 20th century and which reached its apotheosis in J. M. Barrie's *Peter Pan, or The Boy Who Wouldn't Grow Up*, the original play version of which was first performed in 1904. Barrie captures the early 20th-century *Zeitgeist* which helped to usher in the 'century of the child', giving rise to a celebration of childhood imagination and creativity. Evidence of the continuing importance given to childhood is found in the discourses of modernism and the symbolic power assigned to children in the postwar period, when they represented hope for the future after two world wars and the entry into an atomic age. Since 1989 the United Nations Convention on the Rights of the Child has sought to uphold children's rights to have their basic needs to survive and thrive protected. The changing ideas about children and childhood evident in this brief summary are charted in writing for children.

For the first half of the 20th century, a very particular view of childhood dominated Anglo-American children's literature: child characters in, and the implied child readers of, children's literature were, with very few exceptions, prepubescent, white, middle class, and living in families with two heterosexual parents – and often some kind of domestic help – in a patriarchal culture. Childhood was strongly associated with nature, and children in books were regularly shown as highly capable, whether tramping and camping, sailing and riding ponies, or solving crimes. Often they were unsupervised for days on end. For the most part, childhoods in children's literature were shown as largely free from care or want, underpinning the sense of nostalgia for childhood in some of the most enduring books written between 1900 and 1950, among them Kenneth Grahame's *The Wind in the Willows* (1908) and the *Pooh* books of A. A. Milne (1926, 1928). This tone is more frequent in British books than in those from the USA, perhaps reflecting both Britain's longer and more costly engagement in two world wars and the winding up of its empire in tandem with the international ascendancy of America. Nostalgia for childhood, then, can be equated to a greater cultural sense that the changes associated with modernity were severing links with the past.

20th-century developments

By the middle decades of the 20th century, nostalgia was no longer a dominant refrain in writing for children. One reason for this may be because childhood itself was being prolonged: school leaving age was raised in both the UK and the US, meaning that more children remained financially dependent on their parents for longer and, at least in part a reaction to these adjustments, teen culture was born. Following publication of J. D. Salinger's *The Catcher in the Rye* (1951), the first books specifically written for teenagers started to appear on children's lists in the US, followed, after a delay, in the UK. The first books for teenagers such as S. E. Hinton's *The Outsiders* (1967), tended to reject the carefree model of youth and, in line with influential studies such as Erik Erikson's *Childhood and Society* (1950), concentrated instead on the problems that confronted the young and their struggles to become independent. Moreover, children's literature, including films, television, and other sources of information and entertainment used by the young, was starting to introduce ideas and provide vicarious experiences of a kind that had previously been regarded as outside the sphere of childhood. This led some to claim that far from being extended, childhood, as measured by lack of experience, was in fact disappearing.

What was not disappearing, though it was certainly being challenged in mid-20th century children's literature was the white, middle-class world of happy heterosexual families. From first readers and fairy tales through YA fiction, the pages of children's books, comics, and magazines began to be filled with children and young people of different backgrounds, ethnicities, and latterly sexualities. New prizes and curricula supported these changes. John Rowe Townsend's *Gumble's Yard* (1961) shows abandoned, working-class children living in crowded urban conditions trying to support themselves and avoid being taken into care. This is an example of how the whirligig of time eventually brings at least some aspects of publishing back full circle: in many ways, Townsend's plot sounds like something the RTS could have published a century earlier. Stylistically, however, *Gumble's Yard* is indisputably of the 20th century, as are the hard-hitting scenes in American Rosa Guy's novels, *The Friends* (1973) and *Ruby* (1976), about a girl whose family moves from rural Trinidad to Harlem, where her mother dies, her father becomes physically abusive, and she must deal with prejudice and life on the streets of a modern US city.

As well as including more kinds of children in their work, children's writers began to use a variety of modes – realism and fantasy, tragedy and comedy – to confront a range of topical issues. Anne Fine's *Bill's New Frock* (1989), in which schoolboy Bill Simpson wakes up one morning to discover that he has become a girl who wears a frilly pink frock to school, is a comic but telling response to gender inequality; Robert Cormier's *We All Fall Down* (1991) deals with the tragic consequences of random teenage violence and vandalism; *Falling* (1995, English translation 1997), by Belgian writer Anne Provoost, explores the relationships between the secret betrayal of Jews to the Nazis during the Holocaust and the current rise of right-wing groups in a small town in France, while David Levithan imagines a gay utopia in *Boy Meets Boy* (2003). As these scenarios indicate, writing for children now reflects many different childhoods and experiences of adolescence in many kinds of families – single-parent, same-sex, and blended, as well as traditional nuclear families.

This is not to imply that the job of making children's literature representative is now complete. Even in countries with well-developed publishing industries, there remain many groups that are at best under-represented. In North America, for instance, there is only a small body of children's literature about, and even less by, indigenous peoples. One possible explanation for this is that their understanding of how to tell stories is so different from that of the dominant culture that editors may not recognize that if indigenous writers offer stories for publication, editors may not recognize them *as* stories; if they do, they may not back them on the grounds that they are unlikely to sell. If an indigene story is published, the kinds of changes it may undergo in the process – from editing to illustration – may so significantly alter the original that it is no longer a valid part of that culture. Whether such changes are unthinking or deliberate, the consequences are the same. In countries that have little in the way of a children's literature infrastructure or where many languages are spoken, as in parts of South America, Africa, and India, economic and logistical problems may prevent groups from participating in the creation of narratives for children. Almost invariably, members of the dominant culture in any country will be the principal gatekeepers – creators, publishers, educators, librarians, parents – of children's literature, and what they choose to offer will inevitably be influenced by their own understanding of and aspirations for childhood and literature.

For many children and young people today, the Internet may provide a way past many such gatekeepers, the most recent and far-reaching manifestation of the extent to which, over the course of the last century, an increasingly significant part of growing up has involved new media and information technologies. Chapter 3 looks in detail at the changes to reading and writing practices these are engendering, but no history of children's literature would be complete without some discussion of how, and how far, writers and publishers have engaged with the new ways of telling stories and creating texts successive new technologies have made possible.

Contemporary children's narratives and new media

An important aspect of the long history of children's literature concerns how writers, illustrators, and publishers have regularly experimented with new ways of producing children's literature cheaply and attractively. From the days when illustrations had to be coloured in by hand to today's lavishly illustrated picture books, one ambition of children's publishers has been to make books as colourful and attractive as possible as inexpensively (and profitably) as possible. This means that children's literature has often been early to experiment with new print technologies and innovations in paper engineering for creating novelty books such as harlequinades, pop-ups, and books with other kinds of movable parts. The dividing line between books, toys, and games has often been a fine one, and as well as leading to new ways to present print products to children, this has impacted on how stories are told. This kind of impact was clearly seen in the range of 'choose your own adventure stories' that were briefly popular in the 1980s and owed much to the formats and storylines of role-playing games such as 'Dungeons and Dragons'. These simple books offered readers multiple possible plotlines and outcomes, determined through a combination of chance (the throw of a die) and strategy.

The emergence of new media has also influenced the forms, formats, and narrative techniques of writing for children. Children's stories have been adapted for film and television, written to be read on radio, recorded on vinyl, audio tape and CDs and been conceived as CD-ROMs, electronic and online fictions. Each new medium has had its impact on how stories are written, how and where they are encountered, and even what it means to read. The dynamics of this relationship are the subject of

23

Chapter 3, but it is important to end this historical overview by making two points. The first is that for some time those who work in the area of children's literature have broadened their interests to take account of all formats in which young people encounter narratives, whether on the page, on screens, on the stage, in lyrics, from oral sources, or any other medium or vehicle. The second point concerns the role of children in producing children's literature.

As this brief history has shown, children's literature has traditionally been written by adults for children; it is a commonplace of children's literature criticism that unlike other forms of writing, children's literature is defined by its audience rather than such things as genre, period, approach, or who writes it. Historically, children have not written what has been *published* as children's literature because they had little access to the equipment necessary to do so and, even when regard for childhood imagination was at its peak, it was generally assumed that they had too little experience of the world or the craft of writing to have anything to say or to say it interestingly. In fact, children have always been *producers* of stories, riddles, verse, jokes, and other materials (including novels, poems, plays, and other more obviously literary creations), and in an age of desktop publishing, fan fiction, and other forms of online publication, children and young people are finding ways of writing for a public beyond their immediate family, friends, and peers. It is too soon to tell what kind of impact this will have on our understanding of what constitutes children's literature, but it may play a key role in rethinking the usefulness of the label, at least with regard to the academic study of writing intended for the young.

Writing *for* children

In the course of describing the kind of material that has been considered children's literature at different times and how this has changed, some characteristics associated with writing for children and young people have emerged; before going on to look at other developments in the field, it is worth looking at dominant tendencies in narratives for children and young people and how these relate to images of children, childhood, and adolescence.

Despite the vagaries around children's literature and its readers, over the years there has been quite a lot of agreement about what makes a text 'for children' at the levels of style and content. Having analysed the way a number of influential writers of classic children's fiction establish a relationship between narrators and readers, Barbara Wall (1991) concludes that the way adult writers address child readers is analogous to the way adults speak to children, and affects tone of voice, lexis, register, and the amount of detail contained in descriptions and explanations. She identifies three modes typically used in writing for children. The first is double address in which narrators move between addressing child readers and the adults assumed to be reading with them or otherwise monitoring the reading process, often appearing to talk over the heads of the children and to collude with the adults. Single address exclusively addresses child reader while dual address succeeds in addressing both child and adult readers simultaneously and equally, resulting in a satisfying reading experience for both. Attending to Wall's categories of address can be useful in determining how far a book assumes a child readership, and helps to track changes in adult–child relationships in texts over time. As seen in some of the historical examples discussed above, early writing tended to use double address – to the point of including specific sections for adults. From the 20th century to the present, single address has tended to dominate writing for children who are reading books independently. Picture books, which are often read to children by an older person, often employ dual or double address, while dual address is a defining feature of crossover writing.

Address is not the only difference between writing for children and writing for adults. In a frequently quoted comparison of the two, Myles McDowell concludes that:

> Children's books are usually shorter, they tend to favour an active rather than a passive treatment, with dialogue and incident rather than description and introspection; child protagonists are the rule; conventions are much used; the story develops within a clear-cut moral schematism...children's books tend to be optimistic rather than depressive; language is child-oriented; plots are of a distinctive order; probability is often discarded; and one could go on endlessly talking of magic, fantasy, simplicity, and adventure.

Evidence that supports McDowell's summary has been provided by the Danish scholar Torben Weinreich (2000), who demonstrates that the process of adapting adult texts for children involves making them shorter, simpler, and often adding illustrations. Perry Nodelman concludes the first chapter of his detailed analysis of children's literature, *The Hidden Adult: Defining Children's Literature* (2008), with a longer but substantially similar list to McDowell's. As he goes on to say, however, it is important to distinguish between simple and simplistic writing, for many apparently simple children's books say thought-provoking things with elegant, sometimes deceptive, simplicity. For example, E. B. White's *Charlotte's Web* (1952) and Raymond Briggs's *The Man* (1992) engage subtly and philosophically with, among other issues, death and marginalization respectively (see figure 13). Nor are all children's books simply written: Russell Hoban's *The Mouse and His Child* (1967), William Mayne's *Cuddy* (1994) and Justine Larbalestier's *Liar* (2009) are stylistically demanding for readers of any age or level.

Until the late 20th century, there was an unwritten agreement that children's books would not include sex, bad language, or gratuitous violence, on the grounds that writing for children is part of the socializing process and so ought to set good examples and help readers learn approved ways of behaving that are likely to help them lead successful and fulfilling lives. Depressive endings too tended to be shunned, on the assumption that the young need to feel confident about the future and their ability to overcome obstacles. As ideas about childhood have changed, consensus over these attributes has largely broken down, particularly for the older readers who for most of its history were not considered as part of the intended audience for children's literature. Incorporating writing for teenagers challenged many long-held assumptions about children's literature; as a consequence, there are now many stylistically complex children's books that include sex, swearing, and random violence, and which end bleakly. As the age range catered for moves steadily upwards and crossover fiction becomes more common, the label 'children's literature' is increasingly problematic.

Contributing to problematising children's literature is the fact that new writing exists alongside the accumulated body of writing for young readers; for instance, many children's publishers have extensive backlists which often include 'classics' such as *The Children of the New Forest* (1847), *Little Women* (1868), *Pinocchio* (1883), and *The Secret Garden* (1911) written, when ideas of childhood were very different. The differences are not just about how children are understood; to modern eyes, the way many older works traditionally included in histories of children's books are written is often far from short, simple, active, and child-orientated. Obvious examples are those books children annexed when there was little else for them to read – books such as *The Pilgrim's Progress*, *Gulliver's Travels*, or *Ivanhoe* (1819). Books that *were* written for children and were extremely popular with young readers in their day further complicate the picture. An example is Elizabeth Wetherell's, *The*

Wide, Wide World (1850), a work of epic proportions and prodigious piety. The fact that today many of these works are read, if they are read at all, almost exclusively on university courses has opened up debate about whether it is still legitimate to regard them as children's literature.

On the other hand, attempts to ensure that texts for children are suitable on the grounds of simplicity of language and style have regularly foundered: what do you do, say, about Beatrix Potter's still much loved *Tale of Peter Rabbit* (1902) in which the sparrows *implore* Peter to *exert* himself after he is caught by his buttons in Mr McGregor's gooseberry net? (Some American educationalists have assessed the vocabulary in Potter's tale as appropriate for those from seventh grade to college.) Length is equally problematic; while many children's books today are shorter than those in the past, the popularity of the *Harry Potter* books, which regularly exceeded 400 pages (the final volume reached nearly 900), opened the door for many lengthy fantasy series for children.

Given the range of material classified as children's literature in histories of the subject, it is not surprising that it has proved impossible to come up with a coherent way of describing and delimiting it. Ultimately, many of those working in the field agree with John Rowe Townsend, children's author and critic, who in 1971 concluded that 'the only practical definition of a children's book today . . . is a book which appears on the children's list of a publisher'. This pragmatic approach works rather less well now that books may appear on both adult and children's lists – as have Salman Rushdie's *Haroun and the Sea of Stories* (1990), Ian McEwan's *The Day Dreamer* (1994), most of the novels of Jane Gardam, and, of course, the crossover novels of J. K. Rowling, Philip Pullman, and Mark Haddon that have already been mentioned. It seems that if a definition for children's literature is to be found, it may depend less on the way a text is written and what it is about than on its relationship and construction of children and childhood. This is the conclusion reached by Perry Nodelman, who reminds us that children and adults are different, and that just as children's needs need to be taken into account by doctors, psychologists, teachers, architects, and fashion designers, so they require different things in what they read. However, what children require is determined by adults on the basis of recollection, observation, interaction, and a pre-existing body of information, received opinion, and images about children and childhood.

The child in and outside the book

Even though the terms 'child', 'childhood', 'children', and 'adolescence' are regularly used in relation to children's literature, there is no monolithic version of any of these terms or a single vision of childhood behind children's literature. While the influence of Romanticism has had a profound and enduring influence on many aspects of childhood in narratives for children, and some sets of characteristics have tended to dominate (children as innocent, lovable, educable, civilizing), there are also child characters that are evil, brutish, savage, and irredeemable. Multiple sets of children and young people are implicated in every aspect of children's literature, from the child characters in the texts to the implied (but imaginary) child readers to actual child readers. While characters and implied readers may in some sense be fixed, actual readers are constantly changing so, when dealing with a book from the past, the term encompasses the original readers, those who are currently reading it, and all readers in between.

As already indicated, in the UK and the US the term 'children's literature' is now shorthand for writing directed at those from roughly 0 to 16 (that is, from birth to the age when a young person is legally able to leave school), but this varies from country to country and has also changed over time. These children come from many backgrounds, and both as members of groups and as individuals will have a range of needs, abilities, and experiences, so just as it was impossible to identify a single set of stable characteristics common to writing for children, so it is impossible to delimit the child in children's literature. Nevertheless, narratives for children address and construct versions of childhood, and in doing so, they influence how children and childhood are understood, not least by the young. Central to this process is the fact that it is adults who create children's literature, and they do so according to their expectations of what childhood should be like. While these expectations can vary considerably from time to time, place to place, and person to person, the fact that the children in children's literature are adult creations has led Maria Nikolajeva (2009) to conclude that there is at least one constant in children's literature: what she calls 'aetonormativity', or the way adult norms have governed the patterns of children's literature, from its emergence to the present day. The power relation may be true, but adult norms are no more stable than those around childhood, so Nikolajeva's observation is more valuable for the sets of questions it engenders than as a defining feature of children's literature.

However it is defined, the rewards of studying writing for children, both as children's literature and as part of other specialist disciplines, are many. To demonstrate this claim, after a discussion of some of the approaches frequently used to study children's literature, the remaining chapters of this *Very Short Introduction* provide examples of areas where research in children's literature is opening up or extending academic debates.

Chapter 2
Why and how are children's books studied?

Children's literature recapitulates, extends, and modifies the range of narratives that make up 'adults' fiction', but not only do those who study it employ much the same body of critical and theoretical approaches, they also customize and add to them. There are, for instance, approaches that focus on the intended audience, others arising from the study of childhood, and those which take into account the interplay between image and text. For the most part, however, writing for the young is studied in precisely the same ways as any other body of texts, though the fact that children's books are categorized on the basis of age rather than period, genre, producers, or other possible categories means that some critical approaches have tended to be used more than others. This chapter is concerned with critics and approaches that have proved particularly useful for the study of children's literature, whatever the age of the implied reader and whatever the format or medium through which it is transmitted. Before looking at how children's literature is studied, it is worth considering what it offers researchers and what can be learned from narratives for the young, past and present.

Adults reading writing for children

When read by adults for the purposes of research and teaching, texts produced for children can be illuminating at a variety of levels. Since all adults were once children and children's books address child readers and usually contain images of childhood, at a personal level they have the potential to re-engage adults with the children they once were. This process may be particularly intense if the texts being read were also read by that individual in childhood – many people experience a frisson when as adults they come across the same edition of a book frequently handled and read when a child. Although initially returning to childhood reading may produce sentimental or nostalgic responses, most adult readers soon over-ride these with more considered critical reactions. Some texts will disappoint because they are poorly written or banal, and while they might nonetheless carry interesting cultural information, they may also give rise to the suspicion in some that being interested in writing for children is itself childish, and that children's literature is something to be outgrown and left behind rather than something meriting serious study. Bad writing and banality are not unique to children's literature, but it is not uncommon for adults to write in a regressive and infantile way about and for the young. This is the charge made against Henry Vaughan's evocation of childhood by T. S. Eliot:

Children's Literature

> ... we can, if we choose to relax to that extent, indulge in the luxury of the reminiscence of childhood; but if we are at all mature or conscious, we refuse to indulge this weakness to the point of writing or poetizing about it. We know that it is something to be buried and done with, though its corpse will from time to time find its way up to the surface.

Eliot's image of childhood as a buried corpse may jar, but his recognition that the corpse periodically finds its way to the surface acknowledges that our childhoods continue to be implicated in the mature selves we become – a very good reason to re-examine them, and one reason why psychoanalytical critical approaches are frequently used to make readings of children's texts.

One route back to childhood is through the books, comics, magazines, and other materials read then, but this does not mean trying to read as the children we once were. Indeed, children's literature studies specifically eschew this kind of retrogressive luxuriating. Those who do look to themselves or other known children as examples of child readers generally do so in an attempt to discover why certain texts have particular power in childhood and what this reveals. Maria Tatar's *Enchanted Hunters* (2010), for instance, is interested in the way young readers lose themselves in books – what it is about children as readers and the books produced for children and young people that makes them so effective at taking some children out of reach of the world around them. In *The Child that Books Built* (2002), his memoir of being a reading child, Francis Spufford reveals himself to have been precisely the kind of child reader who interests Tatar. He remembers being 'sealed to the outside so that [his reading self] could open to the inside', producing what he calls 'catatonic reading'.

While both Tatar and Spufford look at the effects of texts on individual child readers, most of those who work in this area, with the exception of some educationalists (see the section on reader response criticism below), are more concerned with what texts for children reveal about when, where, or by whom they were produced. This may mean looking at, for example, attitudes to exploration and colonization in 19th-century adventure stories, or to same-sex parenting in 21st-century picture books. As the historical overview in Chapter 1 shows, children's texts are as capable of opening up ideas about the 'childhoods' of countries as they are about personal childhoods. Indeed, some of the qualities identified in the discussion of what children's literature is (particularly that for pre-teens) – its bias towards relatively simple constructions and close connection to the education system, for instance – mean that ideological positions and agendas are often more overt than they are in texts for adults. This can make writing for children a source of historical information about everything from everyday life – many children's books, poems, and stories are, after all, set in homes, nurseries, and schools and involve such mundane activities as going shopping and doing chores – to topical debates at a given moment. Studying children's books, then, can be a way of contemplating a past self or a collective past, but these are just some of the reasons why studying literature for children can be so rewarding.

Setting and bending norms

Because its primary medium is language, and in the course of learning to read children are acquiring much of the vocabulary and many of the concepts they use to think about themselves and the world around them, writing for the young has considerable potential to influence what its intended readers regard as normal, good, acceptable, important, unjust, or to be feared. This makes children's texts valuable sources for those interested in ideological shifts and cultural change. The extent to which children's literature is intellectually and socially formative is often unacknowledged, though in the second half of the last century, children's literature's role in perpetuating gender, class, and racial stereotypes generated heated debates and campaigns to combat these tendencies. Not for the first time, writing for the young was mobilized in support of radical campaigns.

Because the formative nature of children's literature is largely unrecognized or disregarded outside of classrooms, it has the potential to fly beneath the radar of both cultural and personal censors. This is a paradox, since at one level, children's literature is highly regulated: those involved in bringing children and texts together tend to be vigilant about many aspects of writing for the young, leading to the kinds of self-regulation about language and content already discussed. When individuals and groups believe a text transgresses understood boundaries, they can be powerful in their opposition to it, as American writer Judy Blume has discovered. Several of Blume's books have offended the self-appointed guardians of children's literature, but it was her 1975 novel

Forever, which features a teenage couple having sex, an abortion, and a failed suicide by a character who fears he is gay (all unrelated), that has resulted in Blume's being one of the most banned writers in the US.

Forever explicitly challenged convention; more often, children's books are less overt in the way they pose subversive questions about culture and explore issues, attitudes, and desires that might not be considered suitable for children. Sometimes writers and/or illustrators are themselves unaware of what it is they are suggesting; this was particularly true before Sigmund Freud provided a vocabulary for discussing the psyche. There are many readings of classic texts such as *Alice's Adventures in Wonderland* and *Peter Pan* that suggest their writers felt able to explore aspects of themselves when writing for children that they would not have included in their works for adults. Alternatively, writers may specifically seek to address juvenile audiences because they want to shape the rising generation by encouraging them to see things outside the norms of the dominant culture or to foster officially sanctioned new ways of thinking and behaving. Writers in the 17th century used children's books to disseminate ideas about religion, behaviour, and social life; in the 18th century, new scientific and political ideas were disseminated to the young through their books and periodicals; Victorian reformers encouraged religious values, temperance, and charity for poor children in the pages of children's fiction; while during the McCarthy era in the US, children's literature became a place where some of those out of favour with the conservative establishment nurtured progressive views of society.

The expanding field of children's literature studies

Although all the critical and theoretical approaches appropriate for the study of texts can be used to analyse works for the young, some have proved particularly productive. The remainder of this chapter looks at the most influential of these. It is worth noting

4. See facing page for caption

4. This story uses a simple text and accompanying paper doll to teach child readers the virtues of obedience and humility

that until the 1990s, there were relatively few critical studies of children's literature, and so before then it is possible to discuss individual critical texts. By the 21st century, reflecting increased interest, status, and activity in children's literature studies, the numbers of publications in the field have proliferated, making it more representative to concentrate primarily on trends rather than individual works. The tremendous activity in scholarship about children's literature is testament to its attractions, not the least of which is the fact that it offers much virgin terrain – there are many writers, texts, formats, bodies of work, and even periods that have received little if any attention. Considerable work is still to be done on the bibliographical history of children's literature, too. Some sense of its richness as a resource emerges through a survey of the major critical texts and trends in children's literature studies.

Early approaches

Critical responses to children's literature began to appear regularly during the 19th century. The *Guardian of Education*, the first journal to carry serious reviews of children's books, was established in 1802 by the formidable Mrs Sarah Trimmer – mother of 12, writer, critic, and educationalist. As its title suggests, the *Guardian of Education* was concerned to protect children by ensuring that the kind of education they received was wholesome. The existence of such a publication reflects concerns about the important but volatile nature of reading that intensified over the course of the 19th century. Those with the mechanisms of taste and self-control (deemed to be almost exclusively well-educated, wealthy, adult males) were allowed to read freely, but it was thought the poor, women, and children – especially girls – needed to have their reading regulated. In the second number of her journal, Mrs Trimmer spells out the importance of ensuring that children read only what responsible adults have approved:

> Children should not be permitted to make their own choice, or to read any books that may accidentally be thrown in their way, or offered for their perusal; but should be taught to consider it as a *duty*, to consult their parents in this momentous concern.

The fact that it was a woman who set herself up as the authority on children's literature is significant, for it calls into question one of the master narratives of children's literature studies, which is that it was largely men who conceived and controlled the early years of publishing for children. The founding fathers are usually held to be John Locke and Jean-Jacques Rousseau, whose theories about children, education, and civilization, especially as set out in *Some Thoughts Concerning Education* (1693) and *Émile* (1762) respectively, dominated child-rearing and children's education for much of the 18th and 19th centuries, and John Newbery, who is credited with leading commercial publishers into the new terrain of children's literature. However, this version of the birth of children's literature neglects the many women who were instrumental in creating early reading materials: Chapter 1 refers to the contributions of Mary Cooper and Jane Johnson, and there were also women writers, such as Sarah Fielding, author of what is arguably the first school story, *The Governess* (1749), and Maria Edgeworth, whose first work for children, *The Parent's Assistant*, appeared in 1796.

Sarah Trimmer is, then, just one of many women who shaped publishing for children in its early years, in this case through her work as a critic. Trimmer's strong views against fairy stories and in favour of Christian rationalism have been used to present her as a dour figure who would have children read only tedious materials, perpetuating another widespread misconception: that the women who wrote or vetted children's literature in the 18th and 19th centuries were a 'monstrous regiment' of kill-joys with little ability to tell an entertaining story, while men such as Edward Lear, Charles Kingsley, Lewis Carroll, and George MacDonald ushered in the delights of fantasy, nonsense, and child-friendly fictions. As has repeatedly been shown (see sections on historicist and gender-based approaches below), this account of the development of children's literature does a disservice to 18th- and 19th-century women and their writing.

For the most part, early commentaries were addressed to parents as prospective purchasers of the material their children would read and, in line with Trimmer's approach, they tended to focus on whether what was being published for children was likely to do good (for instance, teaching manners and promoting virtuous behaviour) or harm. Advice on what constituted harmful reading tended to be more complicated than that on how to choose beneficial books. Early critics generally assume a middle-class audience (arguably the same is true today), and the type of material considered harmful varied according to the class and sex of the reader. So, for instance, it was thought girls' purity could be damaged by worldly books, though these same works could help prepare boys for the risks and decisions associated with being male. It was feared too much reading by working-class children would distract them from their work and perhaps introduce them to ideas that would make them unfit for their position in society. By contrast, approved reading – largely the Bible, religious tracts, and later the kinds of fictions produced by the religious publishing houses – would guide them towards appropriate views and encourage them to maintain the status quo. Overall, the first critics of children's literature agreed that childhood and adolescence represent the time of maximum learning, when character is formed, and therefore, as Edward Salmon put it in *Juvenile Literature As It Is* (1888), that it was impossible to 'overrate the importance of juvenile literature' on the national character and culture.

Critics in the 19th century had a shared view of the importance of children's literature, but the first sustained attempt to consider children's literature as a body of work was F. J. Harvey Darton's *Children's Books in England: Five Centuries of Social Life* (1932). Darton shifts the focus of criticism from parents to those with a scholarly interest in publishing for children in a history underpinned by bibliographical detail and organized by categories. He also reads the development of children's literature as one which begins with a dry, controlling didacticism that is only relieved when Lewis Carroll's *Alice* (1865) champions 'liberty of thought'. The pattern and structures Darton set continue to influence understanding of the development of children's literature, though from the 1960s, a division emerged between those who were interested in analysing texts, often using the expanding body of critical theory that was being taught and applied in academia, and those who concentrated on pure bibliography. As children's literature studies have become a recognized part of academic teaching and research, the number and kinds of analyses and bibliographies are rapidly expanding. This is not the place to enumerate the work of all the individuals who began mapping the development of writing for children; however, it is important to note that this was undertaken by a mixture of collectors, booksellers, librarians, teachers, publishers, writers, illustrators, enthusiasts – especially of individual writers and genres – and some lone academics whose interest in this area was rarely valued by their colleagues and institutions. Between them, they developed an infrastructure for the study of children's literature, not least in the form of collections, publications, and exhibitions.

If Darton pioneered a book-centred way of approaching the study of children's literature, Paul Hazard, Professor of Comparative Literature at the Collège de France, urged a child-centred approach. His survey of children's literature in Europe and America, *Les livres, les enfants et les hommes* (1932; translated as *Books, Children and Men* in 1944) gives expression to early 20th-century investment in childhood imagination as a rejuvenating force, and to the hope that the 'universal republic of childhood' would triumph over national allegiances. Hazard saw children's books as central to this process, claiming that if children learned about each other through reading each others' books, this would build international understanding and, he hoped, bring an end to conflicts. Although many involved professionally with bringing children and books together were attentive to Hazard's vision, and some key organizations (IBBY, the International Board on Books for Young People), institutions (the International Youth Library in Munich), and prizes (the Children's Peace Literature Award) perpetuate his ideals, in terms of how children's literature is studied today, his greatest legacy is in comparative children's literature, a discipline he founded. The fact that this is a small field which is more actively pursued in non-Anglophone countries points to the largely one-way traffic in the movement of children's books between countries. While it has always been the case that many more children's books in English were translated into other languages this pattern became increasingly pronounced in the second half of the 20th century and has been exacerbated by the ubiquity of English.

Although this study does not look in any detail at the way children's literature is investigated by those involved in children's education, particularly during the 1960s and 1970s, it was often teachers and those who trained them who were most alert to both the high quality and innovation of writing for children and some of its failings. The cross-fertilization between literary, pedagogical, and theoretical approaches, as well as the interdependence between British and North American scholarship, are embodied in the journal *Children's Literature in Education*. Founded in 1970 and jointly edited in North America and the UK, this journal contains examples of all the theoretical approaches discussed in the remainder of this chapter.

Psychoanalytic and psychological approaches

Among the first uses of theory consciously to be applied to children's literature focused on the child's inner world. While psychoanalytic theory alone tended to be used in adult literary criticism, writing for children frequently drew on models and insights from both psychoanalysis and child psychology. The particular affinity between these disciplines and children's literature owes much to the ancient tradition of using stories to help children understand themselves and those around them. Stories that engage with children's fears, anxieties, angry reactions, and 'naughtiness', and offer advice about managing them, span the history of children's literature. For instance, Sarah Fielding's *The Governess* (1749) begins with a quarrel among the girls in Mrs Teachum's Little Female Academy. They learn to overcome their individual shortcomings and uncontrolled passions and coexist harmoniously when each tells a confessional story to the others. The way this book discloses and gives narrative form to hidden aspects of the self has much in common with psychoanalysis, though the discourses used in Fielding's story are embedded in then contemporary concerns such as self-control and Christian duty.

More than a century later, but still before a scientific vocabulary and set of concepts for talking about the psyche had evolved, Mary Louisa Molesworth's children's stories show great understanding of why children behave as they do. For example, *The Cuckoo Clock* (1877) looks at the effects of bereavement, loneliness, and boredom on the fantasy life of young Griselda, while *Sheila's Mystery* (1895) deals with an acute case of sibling rivalry. By the middle of the 20th century, much writing for children draws on understanding both of the psyche and of the child's mind and inner world as explained by child psychologists. Sometimes, as in the case of Catherine Storr, children's writers were also practising psychologists. The extent to which creative and clinical interests began to be intertwined is evident in *The Cool Web* (1977), a collection of essays which brings together insights from writers, illustrators, literary critics, psychologists, librarians, and educationalists. Educational psychologist Nicholas Tucker's *The Child and the Book: A Psychological and Literary Exploration* (1981) added to this approach specific links to the theories of child development developed by Jean Piaget. By the turn of the 21st century, a considerable body of sometimes highly specific critical analysis employing a combination of psychoanalytic and psychological methods had been amassed. Some of this is written by practitioners, such as child psychotherapists Margaret and Michael Rustin's *Narratives of Love and Loss* (1987; revised 2001), some by literature specialists, such as Karen Coats's *Looking Glasses and Neverlands* (2004), which applies the theories of Jacques Lacan to a range of children's texts. Both approaches are ultimately concerned with the extent to which writing for children may shape subjectivity, explore psychic identity, and in the process help children and young people understand themselves.

The same can be said of some primary texts that consciously construct tales about children's psychological dilemmas and development. Key examples are Catherine Storr's *Marianne Dreams* (1958), Maurice Sendak's *Where the Wild Things Are* (1963), and Neil Gaiman's *Coraline* (2002). It is significant that in each case, the protagonists enter dream/secondary worlds where they encounter and triumph over frightening figures and scenarios derived from dilemmas in their everyday lives. The importance of both evoking children's fears in the fiction they read and providing reassurance that they will overcome them is central to one of the most influential studies of the relationships between children and reading: Bruno Bettelheim's *The Uses of Enchantment: The Meaning and Importance of Fairy Tales* (1978).

Bettelheim follows Freud closely; his analyses of well-known fairy tales concentrate on symbolism and the crucial role of the Oedipal drama in children's psychosexual development. While his work is criticized for both its reductive application of Freudian theory and its failure to pay attention to either the historical context or indeed the history of the individual stories he analysed, his claim that children need tales that acknowledge their fears – including the fear that they will be overwhelmed by the strong feelings of hostility and desire they harbour inside – has been influential on both those who study and those who create children's literature.

Freud's ideas have cascaded through culture; by contrast, those of his some-time friend and colleague Carl Jung are less familiar. Arguably, however, they have had greater impact on children's literature writing and criticism. Of particular importance is Jung's belief that infants are born with a sense of wholeness that is lost in the course of such things as being gendered, acquiring language, bodily control, and subjectivity – all key measures of social development. Jung's narrative of personal development emphasizes the need for separation and individuation as part of maturation, but sees these as part of a quest to restore psychic wholeness. Many writers – particularly of juvenile fantasy – have also drawn substantially on Jung's system of archetypes – the symbols by which he believed the conscious and unconscious communicate – and the notion that a healthy psyche balances masculine and feminine aspects.

No discussion of this topic would be complete without mention of Jacqueline Rose's *The Case of Peter Pan, or, the Impossibility of*

Children's Fiction (1984). Rose's work is firmly rooted in the re-reading of Freud's work offered by the French psychoanalyst and psychiatrist Jacques Lacan. She regards children's literature as important in the construction of self-identity since the self is a product of language, language is the medium of fiction, and so, while reading, children are simultaneously involved in learning and experimenting with language and constructing their identities. The aspect of her work that has had the greatest impact is her contention that fictional constructions of childhood have their origins in adult needs and desires. This results in an image of childhood that stands in for a cluster of adult desires – for innocence, coherence, and psychic balance – that bear little relation to actual children and childhoods. Rose's interest in Lacan, language, and subjectivity has been taken further by Karin Lesnik-Oberstein (1994) and Karen Coats (2004).

Linguistic, narratological, and stylistic approaches

One of the first monographs to attempt to analyse children's literature on the basis of its stylistic features is Zohar Shavit's *The Poetics of Children's Literature* (1986), which considers how and where children's literature fits into what she refers to as the literary polysystem, or the variously overlapping and hierarchical systems which organize and shape texts at cultural and global levels. Some of Shavit's ideas have been taken up by others, but her decision to use canonical examples from across the history of children's literature creates problems for her analysis since many of the texts she discusses were not originally intended for children.

In *The Narrator's Voice: The Dilemma of Children's Fiction* (1991), Barbara Wall also provides a historical overview to help her identify stylistic criteria which would make it possible to distinguish children's books from other kinds of writing. All the texts Wall discusses were written to be read by children, by which she means readers under the age of 12. She concludes that most of the earliest material included in histories of children's fiction is not, in fact, children's literature because it was not written in a way that was designed specifically to appeal to the young (see the discussion of single, double, and dual address in Chapter 1). According to *The Narrator's Voice*, children's literature as an identifiable body of work can only be said to exist once writers developed specific ways of addressing child readers; doing that depends on there being a coherent understanding of what a child is and how children differ from adults cognitively, emotionally, and physically. Wall concludes that as well as drawing on an emerging image and understanding of childhood, children's literature both consolidates and helps to create the image of the child it addresses.

The next major work to concentrate on language and style, John Stephens's *Language and Ideology in Children's Fiction* (1992), applies techniques from narratology and linguistic criticism (story and discourse, point of view, focalization, narrative voice, closure) in combination with a number of critical approaches to 20th-century children's texts. Stephens's findings are wide-ranging, but perhaps the most influential is his demonstration that the books children and young people read are ideologically potent and tend to favour liberal humanist values.

Sex and gender-based approaches

A significant body of critical writing about children's literature deals with issues relating to both gender and sexual orientation, and it has had a highly visible impact on the writing, appearance, and marketing of children's literature. During the 1960s and 1970s, the extent to which children's literature was implicated in perpetuating gender stereotypes became a hotly debated issue. Initially, concern focused on the representation of girls and how texts tended to adhere to a feminine ideal that disadvantaged them, suggesting girls were less clever, dynamic, and capable than boys. Writers and publishers consciously set out to address this problem, creating guidelines and works that were intended to counter sexism. Ultimately, this campaign resulted in a large and eclectic body of texts that offers many ways of being successful and female. Part of this process involved recognizing that sexual politics could not advance without addressing the representation of masculinity, at which point both critics and writers began to focus on the problems with masculine stereotypes. Some of the most vociferous debates about masculinity took place in Australia, from where there also emerged a number of YA novels that offered new models of masculinity. John Stephens's edited collection *Ways of Being Male: Representing Masculinity in Children's Literature and Film*, the first and most substantial critical work to address the topic, appeared in 2002.

While there have undoubtedly been improvements in the number and kind of texts that resist limiting gender stereotypes over the past half century, it is notable that the 21st century has witnessed a revival of literature that is targeted at gendered readerships and which seems to be reviving earlier ideas about the nature and potential of males and females. Books marketed as 'for girls' tend to be pink, decorated with fairies for the young or fashion accessories for older girls, and often imply that their readers are interested only in their appearance and being attractive to boys. 'Boys' books feature young soldiers or spies or similarly macho characters who display few emotions and concentrate on developing the kinds of physical skills that will allow them to be dominant in most situations. Their pages are filled with fights, machines, scenes of outdoor life, and spectacular bravery.

This return to tradition has come about despite continued critical activity (see, for instance, Kerry Mallan, 2009) and a growing interest in queer theory (Maria Nikolajeva, 2009). While representations of gender may be retrogressive in some aspects of publishing for children, the situation is quite different when it comes to sexuality. There is a steadily increasing number of both primary and secondary works that validate and celebrate the lives and experiences of gay, lesbian, bi, and transsexual characters and readers. Books that feature characters who are not heterosexual encourage their readers to take up an alternative sexuality for the time of the reading – just as those who are not heterosexual are frequently required to do – encouraging understanding that all sexualities are mutable and current systems of classification are crude. Additionally, experiencing the world from the point of view of a character whose sexuality is different from one's own can promote empathy and identification in ways that straightforward information and consciousness-raising exercises rarely do. This is the strategy employed by David Levithan in *Boy Meets Boy* (2003), set in a gay utopia and narrated by the gay protagonist.

Historical and historicist approaches

From Harvey Darton to the present, a substantial proportion of research in children's literature is historical. This may take the form of looking at books, manuscripts, or other printed materials from the past as physical objects produced at a particular historical moment, or analysing competing discourses of power in fiction from the past, or contemplating how writers from earlier times have constructed images of, say, childhood or parenting or gender or war, or studying how the books were produced, sold, or received. For the most part, historical research using children's texts closely matches that done on adult texts, but because the boundaries around what constitutes children's literature are so large and porous, there are some differences.

Working on adult literature tends to involve looking almost exclusively at literature in the form of printed texts – adaptations for stage and screens are seen as specialisms, if not entirely separate areas of study – and there is little, if any, debate about what constitutes adult literature. With children's literature, however, there are a number of conundrums, most arising from the failure to agree on a single definition of what children's literature is. When dealing with works from the past, this can lead to questions about how far it is right to regard a text such as *The*

Pilgrim's Progress as an example of children's literature, since it was not written for children and for almost a century has rarely been read by children (and then almost always in special juvenile versions). Does it still count as children's literature? Or what about the many toys that took – and indeed take – book form: paper dolls, toy theatres, and pop-ups, for instance? Or card games, board games, puzzles, toys, and other ephemera based on books? All of these tend to be found in historic children's book collections and to be written about under the general heading of 'children's literature'.

A final difference about studying works from the past for adults and children needs to be mentioned here. This relates to the image of the child. Historians of children's literature agree that it is important to be alert to how texts construct images of childhood and how these relate to larger discourses and actual experiences of children when the texts were written. The need to recognize the symbolic and cultural meanings of childhood at a given time is, then, an additional demand on those working with children's texts from the past. While some historians of adult literature are interested in their readers, there is no sense that a similar image of adulthood can be identified beyond some basics of sex, class, and ethnicity.

Postcolonial approaches

That this study is centred on children's literature from English-speaking countries is a legacy of colonizing activities. Unsurprisingly, given the histories of invasion and conquest shared by Britain and North America (including Britain's conquest of many parts of North America), there is a long history of writing about the experience of colonization for children. During the 19th and early 20th centuries, this imperial history permeates major genres such as adventure and exploration stories – both the more factual variety written by G. A. Henty, and fantasies such as Stevenson's *Treasure Island*. Despite an abundance of primary materials, the application of postcolonial theory to children's literature is currently relatively limited. One of the earliest examples was Perry Nodelman's essay, 'The Other: Orientalism, Colonialism, and Children's Literature' (1992). Nodelman applies ideas from Edward Said's *Orientalism* to the adult–child relationships found in children's texts and proposes that children's literature is a literature of colonization in which adults colonize childhood.

Of those who have questioned some of Nodelman's conclusions, Clare Bradford is probably most actively engaged in applying postcolonial theory to children's texts. Bradford has, for example, worked on texts for children generated by indigenous Australians, past and present, helping to identify and elucidate characteristics of their storytelling and illustrative practices. In doing so, she shows how they operate outside the systems of knowledge and value characteristic of the Western Europeans who colonized Australia. In her analyses of settler narratives, she has exposed the narrative strategies that taught young British and Australian readers that they were superior to the aboriginals and legitimized the power they were exercising over them. As Bradford demonstrates, writing for children, with its often overt ideologies and tendency to include visual material, can be a very productive focus for the application of postcolonial theory.

Reader response and reception theories

Given that children's literature is essentially defined by its readership, it is not surprising that reader response theory has been attractive to some of those who study writing for children. Educationalists, with their access to and need to engage with real children as readers, have been particularly active in this area, whether they seek to understand how children develop as readers, the strategies they employ to make texts meaningful, or how texts may affect their grasp of ideas and social practices. Accounts of children's responses now span everything from children as readers of picture books to the way children interact when 'reading' computer games.

Initially, reader response research applied to child readers concepts and methodologies from work with adults developed by such figures such as Louise Rosenblatt (1938), D. W. Harding (1962), Norman Holland (1975), Wolfgang Iser (1978), and Stanley Fish (1980). Like reader response work with adults, this has resulted in a division between those who are primarily interested in how children read texts and make meanings, and those who concentrate on how texts construct readers and seek to provoke particular responses. Key areas of exploration centre on how the concept of the implied reader functions in writing for the young; what children bring to texts; how they complete them; what gives them pleasure, and generally how the interpretive communities of childhood function.

One factor that is unique to reader response work with children is age – both how the wide age-span of those classified as readers of children's literature makes it possible to observe how responses to narrative develop from infancy through adolescence, and what kind of differences exist between child and adult readers. What children bring to texts – how they contribute to their meaning – will be different from what adults bring because they have less experience of the world, are likely to know fewer texts, and the texts they know, including those from materials such as comics, television, and school readers, are likely to be different (for instance, in the proportion of images they include) from those usually read by adults. Among other things, their different experiences of texts will affect the nature of the intertextual references to which young readers are likely to respond. Of course, as children age they will move closer to displaying adult reading strategies, but studies have shown marked differences between adult and child responses even as children move into adolescence.

Very young children have not yet learned how to read, so how they set about the task of decoding words and images differs significantly from older readers who have been taught to look for hidden meanings and narrative devices. Much reader response work shows that far from being incapacitated by not having been trained, young readers are highly inventive and effective at making meanings. As they are taught to read, children are frequently required to read in formal contexts or under supervision, often in response to particular protocols in ways rarely required of adults. All of these factors affect response, as do other more general factors such as class, sex, and education; such social dimensions of how young readers make meaning have initiated projects that seek both to understand and to influence how young readers respond to social issues in their reading. Two areas where this kind of work has been active are in attitudes to sexual equality (as in Kerry Mallan's *Gender Dilemmas*, 2009) and racism (see Beverley Naidoo's *Through Whose Eyes? Exploring Racism: Reader, Text and Context*, 1992).

One of the first and most influential applications of reader response theory in relation to children's literature was Aidan Chambers's 'The Reader in the Book' (1977), an essay that applies ideas from Wolfgang Iser to show that children's books construct implied readers by establishing a particular relationship with a narrator in the form of a 'friendly adult storyteller who knows how to entertain children at the same time as keeping them in their place'. One way he demonstrates this is by comparing two versions of a story by Roald Dahl. The first, 'The Champion of the World' (1959), is a short story for adults; the second is *Danny: The Champion of the World* (1975), a novel for children. In many ways, Chambers's work anticipates that of Shavit and Wall, for his analysis indicates that the nature of the narrator–narratee relationship depends on the prevailing understanding of childhood when a text was written. Shavit and Wall both propose that an important part of developing what could be recognized as a discrete body of writing specifically for children was the evolution of a particular way to address child readers. The avuncular but controlling tone Chambers describes is similar to the narrator's voice Shavit and Wall associate with writing that is genuinely for children.

There are other interpretations of the narrator–narratee relationship in children's literature, however. For instance, Chambers, Shavit, and Wall all assume that the text is constructing an implied reader on the basis of a pre-existing idea of childhood, but it is equally possible to argue that texts construct their readers and so have the capacity to affect that idea. This process can be seen in operation in the discussion of historicist and ideologically led approaches to children's literature discussed above.

Child-orientated theories

> ...those of us who are concerned with children's literature need to beware of the trap laid for us by the very concept of 'literature,' and [adult] literary standards that claim to be (or aspire to be) authoritative...if we value [children as readers who make meaning] at all...we have to see them making it within their own culture.

So says Peter Hunt, a critic who has argued persuasively that children's literature criticism needs to avoid making judgements on behalf of children and instead include the voices of children. Hunt's vision of what he calls 'childist criticism' is closely related to reader response, but concentrates specifically on children as readers – including as readers of pictures. Childist criticism is in part an attempt to address what some regard as a weakness in children's literature studies: the tendency to use theories from other disciplines rather than to generate original approaches. This is only a weakness if children's literature is separated off from the mainstream of literature rather than understood as being concerned with how literature addresses younger readers, in which case it has no need of separate critical approaches beyond those based on age.

Childist criticism can usefully be compared with the branch of feminist criticism known as *écriture féminine*, which aimed to mitigate the 'man-made' nature of language by developing specifically female ways of using language, especially in writing. To some extent, childist criticism attempts to address the 'adult-made' nature of children's literature; the analogy is not perfect, however, since children do not write children's literature or critical studies of it. This means that rather than considering children as writers or seeking to imbue writing with a sense of inhabiting a child's body and/or psyche (in fact, these are exercises that have occupied writers for adults including Henry James, James Joyce, and Virginia Woolf), childist critics concentrate on identifying and exploring specific attributes of children as readers of both text and image.

The spirit of childist criticism has infused several key areas of children's literature studies, including attempts to understand how children used and responded to texts in the past (Galbraith 1997; Grenby 2009), and how familiarity with computer games is affecting the way children read picturebooks (Mackey 2002). Ultimately, however, childist criticism is more of a position than a methodology in its own right, and it is persistently troubled by the fact that an adult mediator is almost inevitably required to elicit, synthesize, and present children's reactions and behaviours. Although the extent of adult intervention generally decreases as children age, most of the publicly available accounts of children and young people's critical responses to texts are nonetheless managed and given meaning by adults.

Peter Hunt developed the term and attempted to set out how childist criticism could work, but it was the British writer and critic Aidan Chambers who first called for 'a critical method that will take account of the child-as-reader'. Chambers encourages children to talk about books in a critical way through the creation of reading communities in which readers share enthusiasms, discuss things they find puzzling, identify patterns, and make connections between books. Having gained access to readings of books made by children, Chambers demonstrates that while they may read differently from adults, children are equally capable of formulating thoughtful and insightful responses to texts – the responses that concern childist critics. For Chambers, the differences between child and adult readings tend to be linked to the education system, since before they have learned what is valued by teachers and examiners, children often respond to different aspects of texts than do adult critics. Related to this observation is the suggestion that as relatively new readers who have mastered fewer reading strategies, young readers are often more fully drawn in to what they are reading than are adults. They are effectively reading themselves as much as the texts, accounting for some of the engagement and satisfaction they experience when reading something that to an adult may look banal.

Another study which has much in common with childist criticism is Peter Hollindale's *Signs of Childness in Children's Books* (1997), in which Hollindale proposes that children and adults both have access to what he calls 'childness' or 'the quality of being a child'. This quality is characterized by its ability to respond to change in a way that is often lost or over-ridden in maturity; Philip Pullman makes a similar point in a literary way through his creation of dæmons in *His Dark Materials*, for while children's dæmons are constantly changing, those of adults are permanently settled. Hollindale proposes that children's books create a space where adulthood and childhood can meet and mingle, with adults reactivating aspects of what it was like to be a child – particularly the mutability and potentiality of childhood – while children gain insights into what it is like to be adult. The nature of this dynamic was summed up by the children's writer and illustrator C. Walter Hodges when he observed, 'if in every child there is an adult trying to get out, equally in every adult there is a child trying to get back.

On the overlapping of those two, *there* is the common ground.' The common ground constitutes childness, but the experience of childness differs for the two groups, since children are still negotiating childhood and youth, while adults are recollecting their own childhoods and responding to imperatives from the children they once were and who continue to exist emotionally within them. Unlike T. S. Eliot and others who regard reading children's literature in adulthood as regressive, and in childhood as merely a preparation for reading 'real' books and something to grow out of, Hollindale accords it substantial value. Much of this value for Hollindale resides in the literary qualities of and narrative strategies employed in the texts, and this results in a significant difference in emphasis and critical practice from childist criticism, since Hollindale is less interested in children as readers than in the texts of childhood.

Many other critics have also been interested in the kind of interchange between adult and child afforded by children's literature; for instance, Perry Nodelman (1998) considers how a wide range of books for children and young people provide aesthetic pleasure for what he calls the 'hidden adult' reader. A different understanding of the 'hidden adult' is put forward by U. C. Knoepflmacher and Mitzi Myers in their discussion of 'cross-writing'. They start by recognizing that when writing for the young, authors 'inevitably create a colloquy between past and present selves' (generally past child self and present adult self), but the adult voice is frequently overlooked or unacknowledged and so hidden. The relationship between past and present selves is also explored by Maria Tatar in *Enchanted Hunters* (2009). Tatar is interested in how the texts of childhood affect readers, including how adults remember the experience of childhood reading and differences between reading as an adult and reading as a child. Her research brings together mature readers' recollections of and reflections on their childhood reading experiences, and her conclusions are double-edged. While in many ways this is a celebration of the imaginative power of children's literature, it is also about the susceptibility of the child readers who find themselves in thrall to books and what is taken away from them as they become mature readers. The title of the book says it all, for *Enchanted Hunters* is also the name of the hotel where Nabokov's Humbert Humbert seduces Lolita, subtly changing her relationship with her own inquisitive child self.

Approaching children's literature from the perspective of the child reader opens up some interesting philosophical and ethical debates about the adult–child relationship in and outside the text. An area of children's literature that often raises complex questions is that comprising works with a high visual component, especially picturebooks and graphic novels. For a long time in the West, this was also the body of work that was most easily distinguished from adult fiction, now largely devoid of images, although graphic novels are becoming more popular with adult readers, too. Nevertheless, children's literature is where most work on visual texts has been conducted.

Reading visual texts

Most work on visual texts has concentrated on picture books, in which words, images, and other visual elements largely repeat information, and picturebooks, in which words and visual elements are interdependent (the distinction between the two has only recently become regularized). Particularly in picturebooks, the interaction between words and images is a complex one that rewards careful analysis – even when the words are implied, as in wordless picturebooks. William Moebius (1986) was among the first scholars to attend to the intricacies of reading pictures in literature for children. He devised a set of codes for analysing images in picturebooks which takes account of all aspects of a book – from pictures on endpapers to the size and placement of individual illustrations through intertextual allusions and symbolism to the relationships between words and images. Moebius is concerned with how all aspects of design – perspective, colour, relationships between images, even the thickness of lines in drawings and the way layout and page turns affect tempo – influence meaning. Similar attention to the physical and aesthetic elements of texts informs the work of Perry Nodelman, whose *Words about Pictures: The Narrative Art of Children's Picture Books* (1988) provides detailed readings of individual texts along similar lines to Moebius, although his canvas is much larger. Nodelman also offers a general statement about the word–image relationship in picturebooks: in his view, this is inevitably ironic. Whether or not true of *all* picture books, it is true of most picturebooks, and particularly the many works that display postmodern tendencies. These form the basis of David Lewis's *Reading Contemporary Picturebooks: Picturing Text* (2001), in which Lewis identifies and explains the extent and vigour of the relationship between picturebooks and postmodernism, and through close readings of a wide range of highly complex 20th-century picturebooks, both confirms Moebius and

5. 'Darkness overcomes you' from Shaun Tan's *The Red Tree* (2001). The interaction between the minimal text and Shaun Tan's series of expressionistic paintings helps readers of all ages explore feelings of despair and isolation

Nodelman's claims for the complexity of the form and calls attention to its intrinsic playfulness.

Analysis of picturebooks is a key area where children's literature criticism does not map onto pre-existing work with adult texts, and it is worth remembering that children's literature includes many other kinds of visual texts: illustrated fiction, graphic novels, comics, manga, and, increasingly, electronic narratives including those in the form of computer games. There are specialist studies in each of these areas, and some work has been done to propose a technical vocabulary for discussing such texts. Maria Nikolajeva and Carole Scott's *How Picturebooks Work* (2001) proposes a specific vocabulary for looking at picturebooks and shows how these transcend national and cultural boundaries, while Scott McCloud's *Understanding Comics: The Invisible Art* (1993) offers detailed guidance on how to interpret the conventions of strip comics. As its name suggests, *Comics Scholarship on the Net: A Brief Annotated Bibliography*, offers a bibliography of work relating to comics in the broadest sense. The section on 'Story-telling, Stage and Screen' in Janet Maybin and Nicola Watson's edited collection *Children's Literature: Approaches and Territories* (2009) provides an overview and recommends reading on the kinds of visual texts that make up performance. Margaret Mackey's (2007) research into computer games and narrative is currently the most fully developed work in this area specifically related to children's literature.

Studying children's literature in the future

Recurring themes in this chapter have been the multifarious nature of children's literature and the way it constantly exceeds the purview of 'adult' literature. The eclecticism of its primary materials gives rise to both the strengths (inclusiveness, variety, curiosity) and the weaknesses (breadth over depth, lack of specialisms, insufficient contextual knowledge) of children's literature studies today. Now that children's literature has become a recognized area of research and teaching in higher education, a case could be made for ceasing to regard it as a discrete area and incorporating it within the spread of categories applied to the study of 'adult' literature. Placing children's literature studies within well-developed scholarly contexts associated with particular periods, genres, writers, publishing practice, and/or critical approaches could enhance the status of children's texts and authors, bringing them in from the periphery of academic study. There are other potential benefits from such a change. Currently, most of those who 'specialize' in children's literature are required to have broad interests. Most courses span large historical periods and encompass many genres; similarly, most reference works attempt to cover all the areas and aspects currently classified as children's literature. This situation can work against depth and sustained exploration of materials. Some movement in this direction is occurring, particularly among those working with materials from earlier periods, notably in the areas of medieval, Renaissance, and 18th-century studies.

Although much could be gained from incorporating children's literature into the mainstream of literary studies, there are potential losses too, for good research in children's literature requires good knowledge of its history, texts, and genres, its use of visual elements and constructions of childhood across cultures and periods, and, related to these, elements of style that have evolved specifically in response to the task of writing for the young. For now, such a move seems premature; particularly since, as the following chapter shows, writing for children may be loosening some of its ties with writing for adults.

Chapter 3
Transforming the texts of childhood

Each new generation is inducted into literary tradition in a variety of ways. The process is likely to involve stories that are passed on orally, whether told extemporarily or read aloud. It is undoubtedly part of learning to read, since reading is firmly linked to education and comes with considerable cultural baggage relating to the perceived status of texts and genres, the skills of reading and exegesis, and the value of stories for passing on information about society. Today, many children encounter stories through a variety of media and performances, and children's literature studies is interested in them all as well as the way they interact. For instance, a young child who watches a popular programme such as the BBC's *CBeebies* may first be introduced to Shakespeare's *A Midsummer Night's Dream* when watching the programme, but can then revisit the *CBeebies'* website to read along with the digital book and in due course explore it again through Marcia Williams's comic strip version (*Mr William Shakespeare's Plays*, 1998). Over time, that same young reader may enjoy a graphic novel version (*Picture This* series, 2005), a prose retelling of the story by Leon Garfield (1985), a film adaptation such as director Michael Hoffman's star-studded 1999 offering, or a modern retelling for television – perhaps John Bowker's in the *Shakespeare Re-Told* series (BBC, 2005) – as well as seeing a traditional stage performance and reading Shakespeare's play-text. There are many ways by which the young encounter narratives, but doing so is a fundamental part of socialization for, as media specialist Henry Jenkins observes, 'enacting, reciting and appropriating elements from preexisting stories is a valuable and organic part of the process by which children develop cultural literacy'.

Being introduced to literary tradition – the accumulated stock of stories – is central to understanding culture, but *pre-existing* stories are just part of the process. The reservoir of stories is not stagnant, but constantly refreshed and replenished, so every generation of children is also given *new* stories that speak to current needs, interests, and concerns. Familiarity with new tales and texts is also part of what it means to be culturally literate. Sometimes new stories are made by recasting earlier versions, as seen in the case of *A Midsummer Night's Dream*, sometimes they are entirely new stories for new times; either way, new stories are often the product of interactions with new media.

Children's literature and the evolution of modes

One way in which children's literature differs from literature published for adults is the avidity with which it embraces developments in technology and new media. This is reflected in the fact that while the study of writing for adults tends to regard narratives developed for new media and adaptations of existing texts into different media as ancillary to the study of literary texts, they are integrated in children's literature studies. From the beginnings of commercial publishing, printers and publishers have experimented with new ways to make books and other print items attractive to the young. Often, this depends on industrial and technological developments which result in new or improved ways of delivering text. In the 19th century, such developments included ways to produce and use cheaper papers, the incorporation of more images less expensively, the discovery of economical ways of printing in colour, making inexpensive bindings, and affordable ways to include novelty features such as pop-ups, flaps, volvelles, and other kinds of paper engineering. During the 20th century, the work of re-presenting texts was extended to new media and information technologies, so stories could be delivered in evolving audio and audio-visual forms.

Since the end of the last century, digital media have increasingly been used to deliver narrative in the form of computer games and online texts such as fan fictions or hypertext narratives. This has considerably enlarged the interactive potential of earlier formats, and a drive to increase interactivity continues to underpin many aspects of digital publishing. For a time, however, one sector of the digital market resisted the attractions of interactivity: until recently, e-books have essentially been print books delivered on a screen. One reason for this unembellished transfer from print to screen is price: it is relatively inexpensive to digitize existing word-only texts and manufacture e-book readers with the limited functionality required to read them. Another is the fact that unusually, since new media forms tend to be adopted by younger audiences in the first instance, the first significant audience for e-books was made up of adult readers who wanted the portability of the e-book but the familiar features of the fixed-print book.

The limited capacity for storing heavily illustrated material and the fact that initially the devices were quite fragile and the screens too small to be appropriate for texts with high levels of visual content made the first generations of e-books unsuitable for younger readers. Recently, however, the technology required to provide bigger, more robust screens has become less expensive, and even very young children are starting to be catered for. The result is that the nature of texts is changing to reflect the potential of the medium; as they are directed towards the juvenile market, e-books are introducing both increased visual content and higher levels of interactivity. E-books for young children designed for devices such as the iPad respond to touch and action. When reading *Alice for the iPad*, for instance, tilting the screen makes Alice grow or shrink, while shaking it moves characters' heads.

iPad books often also incorporate games, activities, and opportunities for readers to record their own voices reading the book, entirely changing both the parameters of the texts and the meaning of 'reading to yourself'.

Superficially, it might seem as if the invitations to manipulate text offered by the most recent generation of e-books are merely electronic embellishments of the transformative potential provided by movable parts in conventional paper texts; in fact, they are part of a significant change to the nature of narrative. Currently, this change is most apparent in two areas: new iterations of traditional tales, and crossover fantasy series, which themselves often incorporate and reinflect elements borrowed from myths, legends, sagas, folk and fairy tales. That the oldest forms of literature are receiving cutting-edge treatments is a reminder that through stories, children are simultaneously inducted into literary tradition and taught the skills that will make them fully literate in terms of their own times.

Transliteracy, transtexts, and transition

Once, literacy focused on the ability to read and write, primarily in fixed print and paper-based media. In the 21st century, however, it is necessary to think in terms of transliteracy – literacy that crosses between media and is no longer exclusively text-based. Encountering traditional texts in multiple – including multimedia – versions is an effective way to encourage both cultural and text-related literacy. Children do not have a monopoly on transliteracy, of course, but many adults have become transliterate long after first learning to read and may be less comfortable moving between media. Adults who share electronic texts with young children are often improving their own transliteracy as they do so (developing adult literacy is frequently an added-value aspect of children's literature). Movement between media is often encouraged through remediation (also called transmediation) strategies, meaning the way new media tend to ingratiate themselves with audiences by referencing, mimicking, or even incorporating established media. As one of the most familiar media for delivering stories, print has often been the remediation default. This is particularly true with regard to narratives for children, since childhood is the time when most people learn to read. The alliance between print (usually in the form of books) and new media is evident in examples ranging from Disney film versions of classic fairy tales, which begin with a book that is opened to release the story, to CD-ROM and e-books that mimic the action of turning the page.

Remediation is not just a sop to those accustomed to earlier ways of receiving texts: it also has potentially conservative aesthetic ramifications since adult producers, designers, and technicians will also have grown up with earlier media. Even individuals who have a good technical grasp of what a new medium can do will have internalized ideas about how stories work in the media they know well, and these can limit how far they are capable of experimenting with and exploiting a new medium's storytelling potential. As a general rule, it is those who first meet a medium when young who are most adventurous and ambitious for its use when they in turn become the makers of text and the managers of media. Moreover, because the narrative potential of new media is often most fully explored in materials for the young, even if, with the advantage of hindsight, their first experiences of narrative delivered through a new medium later seem crude, children's texts can be a springboard for innovation. This has proven to be particularly true with the transition to multimedia, where storytelling not only combines several different kinds of media (audio, film, still image, and print) in a single text, but is also dispersed across several forms (the book, the film, the graphic novel, the comic, the animation, the computer game), often as part of media franchises.

To date, the most developed multi-version narratives have been produced for children. One of the first of these to reach public notice grew from the Pokémon phenomenon that began in the 1990s. For the purposes of this discussion, the stories themselves are less interesting than the relationships between the parts from which they are constructed and what these reveal about how multiple versions of texts across media are affecting both the nature of text, and how the rising generation is being encouraged to understand what it means to read.

Narrative networks

There is a long history of producing multiple versions of texts for children. Until now, however, each encounter with narrative has tended to be discrete and self-contained; for instance, while films based on books and books based on films were often experienced by the same audiences, each had also to stand alone and work in terms of its own medium. This meant that often different story products were competing with each other, since not all children would watch, listen to, and read different versions of the same text, and versions were compared and judged against each other. Traditionally, the transfer between media has focused on broadening audiences, usually by appealing to younger and younger markets. A significant change is taking place in the relationship between multiple versions of texts delivered via different media and/or through different formats in a single medium. This change affects both the nature and the audience for multi-version texts.

While children today are born into a multimedia environment, earlier texts and formats have not disappeared, so the opportunity to experience many individual versions of a story still exists, but there is a new dimension to this process. Historically, new versions of texts tended to take the form of adaptations – transferring a story from one medium to another in a way intended to make a satisfying aesthetic experience in its own right. Increasingly, multiple versions of texts are being generated as parts of interconnected and coordinated networks constructed by media conglomerations. In these transmedia networks, the same core story is dispersed and delivered across a range of media and a variety of formats; for instance, as a book, film, graphic novel, computer game and/or body of fan fiction. Instead of a succession of independent re-presentations of a story for different age groups as was seen with *A Midsummer Night's Dream*, versions in different media are conjoined in ways that resemble series narratives, with each component offering new information and insights for broadly the same audiences. Different story products no longer compete with each other, but are increasingly complementary and dynamic, a fact acknowledged by the sharing of assets. So, for example, across a transmedia network a computer game will incorporate footage from the film, the film will reference game play, and if the printed text is still evolving, as is likely if the chain is based on contemporary series fiction, new books are likely to draw on or otherwise acknowledge the way other media elements in the network have developed characters, plots, and settings. At one level, this is about stimulating new patterns of consumption, since each part of the network is also a product and may generate spin-off merchandise, but it also affects the nature of narrative.

The most elaborate transmedia networks have evolved around bestselling fantasy fiction. The *Harry Potter* books of J. K. Rowling exemplify such networks and identify children's literature as a key player in the development of what Henry Jenkins calls 'convergence culture', meaning:

> the flow of content across multiple media platforms, the cooperation between multiple media industries, and the migrating behaviour of media audiences who will go almost anywhere in search of the kinds of entertainment experiences they want.

In converged readings, stories become multisensory combinations of all available media: they are read, played, watched, and heard. What is particularly interesting about *Harry Potter* is that it began with a traditional fixed-print children's book, but over the time

Rowling was writing the series, it was reconceived as a transmedia network. The master *Harry Potter* network consists of books, audio recordings, films, online and computer games, fan fiction, websites, and blogs (there are many other Potter-inspired products and events which interact with the network but do not develop the narrative and so are beyond the scope of this discussion). As the network has grown, each added version has created new opportunities to explore the world of Harry Potter, filling in gaps in the books and offering different points of view. There is also evidence that later books in the series show Rowling's plots and style being affected by her awareness of the other versions of and adjuncts to her books that committed fans were consuming, leading to set pieces and plot devices such as the Marauders' Map that readily transfer to transmedia versions of the books.

Analyses of this phenomenon tend to assume that the books are the original or source texts and that all other ways of encountering the evolving story of the boy wizard and his quest to defeat evil in the form of Voldemort are limited to retelling the story in reduced versions. This is the case made by Andrew Burn (2004, 2006) in comparisons of the same scene from three versions of *Harry Potter and the Chamber of Secrets*. Burn demonstrates that in the transition from book (Rowling 1998) to film (Columbus 2002) to computer game (Electronic Arts 2002) there is not only considerable loss of detail, but also that the character of Harry becomes more action-centred and heroic and less interestingly conflicted, while his companions become less important to his success, wellbeing, and personal development. While the facts are as Burn presents them, his analyses are comparative, focusing on responses to each version individually, so they do not take account of the relationship between parts and the whole in a transmedia network or the collaborative style of reading that it seeks to provoke. As Jenkins explains:

> To fully experience any fictional [transmedia] world, consumers
> must assume the role of hunters and gatherers, chasing down bits

of the story across media channels, comparing notes with each other via online discussion groups, and collaborating to ensure that everyone who invests time and effort will come away with a richer entertainment experience.

The desire to use the Internet to pool information and discuss possible solutions to the puzzles Rowling planted in each story is behaviour originally associated with computer games and is symptomatic of how boundaries between media and different versions of texts are breaking down. Where once reading was an intensely private experience – it happened in response to a printed text in an individual reader's head at that reader's pace, and the kind of responses it generated owed much to the reader's personal life and reading history – those growing up in a multimedia environment increasingly expect reading to involve other people and versions of texts which variously position them as viewers, players, readers, and producers of text. Since a transmedia network like that which has formed around the *Harry Potter* books will include contributions from huge numbers of reader-player-viewer-writers who share information, opinions, solutions, and speculations, those who opt to participate in them no longer experience the books as self-contained, but as part of a creation that is too big and complex for a single medium.

Fully evolved transmedia networks are currently few, and thus far they have tended to concentrate on texts that combine adventure, quest, and fantasy; nevertheless, the way they construct narrative is affecting both reading by and writing for the young in some clearly identifiable ways. The bestselling books of Patrick Carman, for instance, are conceived as mini-transmedia networks. Readers of the *Tracker* series (2010–) reach points in the printed text which send them online to watch video clips and play games that provide information necessary to the plot. Despite the fact that – as has been true of all media when they are first introduced – there is anxiety that transmedia narratives threaten the reading of conventional print media, some of the ways in which reading is being affected have the potential to deepen understanding of how narrative works. For example, they can make it easier for those who are not readily drawn into print-based fiction to make use of skills from other areas of literacy in which they are more proficient. The fusion of media is also enabling ways of writing that are allowing new kinds of stories – stories that reflect the experience of growing up with ever-more versatile information technologies.

The three Is: interactivity, interpersonality, and immersion

Children's first encounters with stories as part of transmedia chains usually begin with television programmes such as *Sesame Street*, *Bob the Builder*, or *In the Night Garden*. The programmes introduce them to characters, setting, and a selection of stories, and are extended through websites that offer activities including read-along stories that resemble conventional picture books: children hear a story and can also see the printed text, which changes colour as each word is spoken. Although similar to picture books, these onscreen versions are likely to include animation, sound, and some hypertext links that allow children to interact with the text by touching or clicking.

The networks include a wide range of products, including DVDs of the television programmes and specially made films, interactive books, computer games, and toys. While they can be enjoyed separately, many are designed to be used in combination, increasing the potential for interaction while creating incentives to buy more products in the network. So, for example, a Bob the Builder doll may incorporate a handset that is linked to a Bob the Builder book; pushing a number prompts Bob to speak phrases that complement the corresponding page in the book. The claims for these transmedia networks show how traditional literacy skills are blending with other kinds of learning and entertainment. For example, in addition to teaching such familiar skills as number, letter, and colour recognition, Button Sound Books, producers of a range of Bob the Builder books and linked products, promise that their young users will also 'learn how to use a microphone, a camera, and how to play the piano and guitar'! These first-stage transmedia networks demonstrate two key elements of transmediality: they are interactive and, because young children require adult help with various aspects of accessing and using the texts, they have an intrinsic interpersonal dimension. Interpersonality is extended if more than one child is participating; Mackey (2010) has shown that children can work together on such texts, transferring decoding and problem-solving skills learned from picturebooks and computer games between the two media. For older children, interpersonal elements are normally experienced through games and online forums that are designed for multiple users.

A third element of transmediality is immersion, usually used to describe the level of involvement of someone playing a computer game. Immersion is an equally valid way of describing the experience of being 'lost in a book', however, and examining the ways in which transmedia chains may enhance or disrupt immersion reveals the extent to which they can complement the reading of conventional, print-based materials. Being fully immersed in a book or film or game is pleasurable, but it is often regarded as a state in which the critical faculties are suspended. The first encounter with a text in a transmedia network is likely to produce a high degree of immersion, but once 'readers' start to move across the network and participate in ongoing discussions about the different manifestations of the text, satisfaction comes from studying, questioning, and testing different parts of the network and attempting to make discoveries that deepen understanding rather than striving for greater degrees of immersion. This raises some interesting comparisons with the goals and strategies used for the teaching of literature.

As they move through the education system, children are required to understand reading as a hermeneutic process: stories, they learn, operate on more than one level and so require interpretation. A common complaint is that stories read in school are ruined by the constant demand that pupils look beneath the surface of the text, pay attention to such things as genre, point of view, digression, changes in tense, elements of style, and the need to fill in gaps in a narrative. Interestingly, many of these features are foregrounded in the process of reading transmedia texts, whether this involves gathering clues about events, actions, characterization, or setting, or experimenting with point of view. Interactive computer games in particular require problem-solving that turns interpretative strategies into concrete activities. Playing a computer game based on a *Harry Potter* book, for instance, makes it possible to change point of view by changing avatars, while the nature of digressions and why these may involve a change in tense is unproblematic for a player who activates a hypertext link and experiences a real-time episode that casts light on a previously hidden feature of plot or motivation.

As games become more sophisticated, they are increasingly making use of complex, carefully researched, and well-written narratives and conveying them through a combination of print materials – the need to read books, letters, messages, diaries, and a variety of other documents for vital information is often a feature of game play. Examples of the attention being paid to the writing of computer game narratives are *Assassin's Creed* (2008) and *Assassin's Creed II* (2009), set in highly detailed and extensive recreations of the Holy Land during the Crusades and 15th-century Italy respectively. These are as much historical adventure stories as games, and their capacity for immersion derives from highly evolved backstories delivered through dialogue and documents and giving rise to the impressively realistic settings. The importance of narrative to the games is apparent from the fact that Umberto Eco, medievalist and novelist among other things, was hired as a consultant on the project. Given Eco's interest in creating roles for readers, requiring them to solve puzzles that are often based on other texts and the activity of reading, and making texts open to multiple interpretations, his enthusiasm for game narrative is, perhaps, unsurprising. Eco's skills as a historian and writer shape the *Assassin* games, but the influence between games and fictions is not one way, and children's writers are increasingly attracted to features associated with game play to produce new kinds of stories and new ways of telling them.

'Book over': new conventions for old fictions

A book that uses narrative conventions associated with computer games to original literary ends is Diana Wynne Jones's *Hexwood* (1993). This complicated, richly intertextual novel begins with a series of sometimes very short chapters that apparently repeat the same events from different perspectives or points in time. The reason for the repetition and the links between the incidents gradually becomes clear: the events are part of a cosmic virtual reality role-playing game used to select the rulers of the galaxy, and the book's structure is based on the game. Just as the 'game over' message tends to be heard several times in rapid succession as new players of games make mistakes, lose lives, and have to start afresh as they explore the game space, so the reader of *Hexwood* restarts the story alongside the character of Anne, who acts as the reader's avatar.

Once in the game, characters lose their sense of identity (in other words, it is highly immersive), merging with the avatar assigned to them. The avatars are all legendary figures including King Arthur, Merlin, various knights of the Round Table, and a dragon-slayer from *Beowulf* – a literary 'dream team'. Since the characters' behaviour is rooted in their literary manifestations, the relationship between books and games is shown to be complementary. In fact, it drives the plot, although in *Hexwood*, the plot is secondary to the telling. Aspects of game play are used to organize the structure and develop characterization – for instance, immersion, replayability, the creation of an alternative world based on a mix of fantastic genres, a battle between good and evil for control of the world, and the use of avatars. Avatars are particularly important since it gradually becomes clear that the correspondences between characters' original literary identities and their avatars have been carefully established and provide clues to characters' pasts, personalities, and powers.

There are many other ways in which the text makes use of the characteristics of computer games, but for this discussion *Hexwood* is interesting because in it Diana Wynne Jones combines patterns, characters, archetypes, and plots from myths, legends, folk and fairy tales with aspects of computer games to create a new story and style from familiar ingredients. Salman Rushdie does something similar in his novel *Luka and the Fire of Life* (2010), a sequel to *Haroun and the Sea of Stories* (1990). *Luka* is about another son of Rashid the storyteller who has to rescue his father. This time, Rashid has succumbed to a mysterious sleeping enchantment, and Luka is on a quest for the Fire of Life which he hopes will wake him and revive his storytelling skills. Like Wynne Jones, Rushdie, who became an aficionado of computer games during the years of the *fatwa*, makes comparisons between the quest format of games and ancient tales, including the kind of fable he is writing in *Luka*. A central theme of the book is mortality, and one way this is explored is by contrasting the different values accorded to life in games, where characters/players have an unlimited number of lives (the kind of restarting that Wynne Jones uses in *Hexwood*), and in real life: Rashid is ageing and Luka is confronted with the knowledge that he will not always be able to be saved.

Rushdie's combination of computer games and traditional tales is primarily about the adaptability of narrative and its importance to all cultures (he draws on a vast array of storytelling traditions in *Luka*). *Hexwood* shares these concerns and underlines stories' ability to comment on society, in this case on the temptations for those with power to play games with the rules. A similar idea is played out in Conor Kostick's *Epic* (2004), a story set in the future on a planet where a multi-player role-playing game – Epic – is used to govern society with the intention of avoiding disputes. A corrupt coterie has secretly taken control of the game to enrich and entrench itself, and the plot is concerned with restoring rightful oversight of the game. To do this, the population first has to understand that the game is being tampered with. This is hard to do, as Epic is highly immersive. Absorption in the game functions as a metaphor for ideology – the colonizers find it impossible to recognize that how they are living is not inevitable.

Change comes when Erik, a young player of the game, impulsively abandons the avatar he has used all his life – one very like himself – and tries something completely different. Virtual Reality (VR) allows him to become Cindella Dragonslayer – an attractive female who uses charm rather than warrior skills. The ability to reinvent the self associated with cyberspace and VR is sometimes a source of anxiety, but repositioning brings new perspectives. As Cindella, new ways of thinking about both the game and everyday life occur to Erik, enabling him and his companions to complete Epic, overthrow the ruling clique, and restore just rule to the planet.

Like *Hexwood*, and *Luka and the Fire of Life*, *Epic* employs a familiar quest structure involving trials and the need to progress through various levels by defeating an assortment of monsters. Much of this text is also written *as* a game, so readers read the commands Erik gives Cindella and then find out what happens when she fulfils them. Where Wynne Jones's and Rushdie's novels largely follow single characters as they work their way through the different levels of their game worlds, *Epic* is won because Erik collaborates with his friends, family, and key members of the community: they forge a convergence culture. Each participates at critical moments, pooling skills and collectively problem-solving. This 21st-century novel, then, validates and makes use of the modes and conventions of computer games and online communities, combining them with elements from traditional tales to develop new ways of telling stories that also offer new ways of thinking about how society is organized and managed.

These three examples show how fixed-print texts are affected by transmediality. They do not belong to transmedia networks, but they are transtexts, for they combine gaming, storytelling, and developments in new media and are part of the process of adjusting young readers' expectations of what narrative is and does. They also indicate why analysing narratives for children increasingly requires academics to look beyond traditional critical approaches to those that are being developed to discuss new technologies. Transtexts for children anticipate some future directions for fiction.

Chapter 4
Genres and generations – the case of the family story

Children's literature is sometimes referred to as a genre on the grounds that it is a distinct category of publishing with recognized conventions that set up certain expectations in its readers. One problem with this view is that children's literature also *contains* all the genres and subgenres used to classify writing, from ancient and broadly based terms such as tragedy, comedy, epic, poetry and drama, to recent and much more specific labels such as chick-lit. In fact, compared to publishing for adults, both the emphasis on established genres and the kind of popular fiction referred to as 'genre fiction' are very high across the range of publishing for children, and many histories, introductions, and reference works dedicated to children's literature reflect this. Most will cover key areas such as the adventure, family, school, and animal story, and probably also fantasy, realism, poetry, historical, and war fiction. Depending on the nature of the work, they may go into more specific areas that nonetheless have clearly defined and stable conventions: the pony story, for instance, or the moral tale. It is not just the amount of genre-led fiction that distinguishes writing for children from writing for adults, however: how it is used, which genres are most prominent, and the effects of writing within genre conventions can also be quite different.

The appeal and status of juvenile genre fiction

The term 'genre fiction' derives from the fact that this kind of writing appeals to large groups of readers by promising and providing familiar reading experiences. It tends to do this through abiding by conventions, employing stereotypes, following formulae, and perhaps resorting to clichéd expressions. The high level of genre fiction that makes up children's literature may go some way to explaining why, as a body of writing, it is often dismissed as undemanding and something to outgrow. However, whether for adults or children, this attitude to genre fiction fails to take account of the fact that genre is less about style than about conventions, which in and of themselves do not result in hackneyed writing or impoverished imagination. In fact, the constraints of convention can be a spur to innovation, provoking writers to explore the possibilities for simultaneously conforming to and transcending genre expectations. Philip Pullman often achieves originality through experimenting with genre: his Sally Lockhart quartet (1985–94) reworks the Victorian sensation novel; *I Was a Rat* (1999) plays with the fairy tale; and *The Good Man Jesus and the Scoundrel Christ* (2010) – not a work for children – is a retelling of parts of the Gospels.

It is important to keep in mind that while writers may consciously be working within well-established genres, for most child readers these texts provide their first experiences of individual genres and so they will not find them familiar or predictable. While younger readers may be aware that certain kinds of books are found in designated sections of libraries or bookshops, it is likely to take some time for them to be clear about the conventions that govern them or to recognize that they themselves are bringing expectations about what kind of reading experience particular groups of books provide.

Becoming familiar with genre conventions is an important aspect of learning to read. Being able to anticipate what is happening can help develop reading confidence, stamina, and satisfaction, while becoming acquainted with genre characteristics is a necessary first step in enabling readers to respond to forms of writing such as parody or aspects of intertextuality. Since many of the narratives children meet are in forms other than print, they may come to understand literary genres in part by drawing on knowledge of other media; for instance, paratextual features such as book covers will often reference the moods, tones, font styles, and imagery of films, highlighting generic conventions that may first have been experienced on the screen. An example of this kind of transfer is evident in the presentation of the enormously popular *Point Horror* books that appeared in the 1990s. These used a stylized logo and dark, atmospheric covers that were clearly drawing on traditions evolved for advertising horror films to promise a similarly frightening reading experience.

More recently, a cover for Stephenie Meyer's *Twilight* (2005) used a strong black background to frame an image composed of white hands clutching a vivid red apple. The colours, font, and image evoke a gothic mood and introduce the characteristically gothic themes of forbidden love and transgressive appetites. Clearly visible veins on the wrists highlight the vulnerability of flesh and prepare the way for the vampire-lover (another stock feature of gothic fiction) at the centre of the plot. Because the original implied readers of *Twilight* were likely to have been familiar with the television series *Buffy the Vampire Slayer* (1997–2003), the motif of the teenage vampire as noble lover would have been familiar, as would the romantic twist on the vampire-gets-girl convention of traditional gothic fiction. The iconography that developed around the books (2005–8) and films (2008–) that make up the *Twilight* saga in turn provided the foundation for the plethora of copycat teen gothic novels Meyer's series spawned, showing how the initiation of young readers into genre conventions, like so much about children's literature, spans and mixes media. It is also an indication of how preferences for genres often differ between writing for adults and children at a given time.

Changing times, changing genres

Most genres straddle both children's and adults' literature, but some are considerably more developed in writing for children, foremost among these being animal and school stories. It is not difficult to explain why these genres (themselves so large that they have well-developed subgenres such as the pony story and the girls' school story) are so strongly associated with children's literature. In the case of the school story, almost all children go to school, and so the setting and the types of incidents associated with it are likely to have immediate appeal and relevance to them. Additionally, since their experience of the world is normally quite limited, the microcosm of the school allows a range of topics and

6. Dorothy Kilner's *The Life and Perambulations of a Mouse* (c. 1783). Kilner was one of the many 18th-century women writers who found new ways to engage child readers by experimenting with point of view and narrative voice; in this case, the story is narrated by a mouse

issues to be explored in a context and at a level they readily understand: the politics of parliament might be confusing and alien, but the politics of the playground are intensely relevant and must be negotiated. It is not surprising, then, that the school story is one of the oldest and most fully developed genres associated with children's literature.

The tradition of animal stories is even longer and more various. *Aesop's Fables* was one of the first books Caxton printed, and there are many animals in folk and fairy tales and religious texts. Writers of the 18th century used animals to teach children their responsibilities for looking after the created world, as in Sarah Trimmer's *The History of the Robins* (1786), and their duties as children and subjects in moral tales such as Dorothy Kilner's *The Life and Perambulations of a Mouse* (c. 1783). Kilner's story initiated the tradition of having an animal tell the story of its own life, giving rise to a subgenre with some notable descendants such as Anna Sewell's *Black Beauty* (1877) and Robert Lawson's *Ben and Me: An Astonishing Life of Benjamin Franklin by His Good Mouse Amos* (1937). There are naturalistic animal stories such as Jack London's *The Call of the Wild* (1903), highly anthropomorphized stories typified by Kenneth Grahame's *The Wind in the Willows* (1908), and fantastic animal tales such as Melvin Burgess's *Tiger, Tiger* (1996), in which a female tiger with supernatural powers saves her species from extinction by temporarily transforming a young boy into a male tiger who mates with her. As these examples indicate, writers of animal stories almost inevitably blur the boundary between fantasy and realism, since the genre requires them to render animals' thoughts in human language. Particularly in the early days of commercial publishing, there was anxiety about such fantastical devices on the grounds that they might make it hard for children to distinguish between fact and fiction. Despite their dependence on the fantastical device of talking beasts, animal stories have been a staple genre of children's literature since the 18th century.

Many reasons for the widespread use of animals in children's literature have been proposed. Critics have, for instance, pointed to the similarities in status between animals and children which make animals effective points of identification for young readers. Domesticated animals in particular may share similarities with children since they are relatively weak, inarticulate, and powerless in relation to adult humans. Another suggestion for why animals feature so often in stories for children and young people is that displacing potentially disturbing issues and behaviours – such things as death, sex, violence, and abuse – from the human to the animal world allows them to be more easily managed. This kind of distancing can work in many ways; for instance, giving animals human speech and rationality holds up the mirror to our own behaviour, enabling young readers to comprehend forms such as satire or to recognize political critique. The animal dæmons in Philip Pullman's *His Dark Materials* provide a variation on this function as they externalize aspects of characters' inner selves. Where people's dæmons are closely linked to their sex, gender, and sexuality, animal characters are often used precisely to minimize the need to dwell on issues such as age, sex, class, and ethnicity. This function can be particularly helpful to illustrators who want to avoid making such information explicit.

It is important to remember that representations of the relationship between children and animals outside children's books are often quite different from those found in stories about animals for children. There is, for instance, little sense of empathy between children and animals in William Hogarth's engraving *First Stage of Cruelty* (1751), and even much 19th-century children's literature includes instructions not to harm animals or steal eggs from birds' nests specifically because it was common for children to do so.

The kinds of social change that have transformed attitudes to animals also affect the status of genres. A good proportion of what is now known as children's literature is made up of genres that were once staples of writing for adults but are now more commonly directed towards children, among them myths, legends, folk and fairy tales, and nonsense literature. According to Jacqueline Rose, children's literature is charged with the care of certain older forms of literary texts as a way of preserving and eventually restoring values perceived as being 'on the point of collapse' in contemporary culture. The fact that children's literature serves as a repository for genres does not mean that they atrophy or become infantilized once they enter the juvenile sphere. Indeed, in *Radical Children's Literature: Future Visions and Aesthetic Transformations* (2007), I argue that when genres migrate from adults' to children's literature they are not just preserved, but restored and rejuvenated. Examples of this kind of renewal can be seen in feminist retellings of fairy tales, the use of nonsense by postmodern writers such as Salman Rushdie, and the mixing of traditional tales to achieve new registers and messages in crossover films such as the *Shrek* series (2001, 2004, 2007, 2010).

Genres in children's literature are culturally sensitive: they mutate or are muted in response to the concerns of society, and sometimes to developments in writing for adults. So, for instance, the children's adventure story was originally associated with and has tended to thrive during times of colonization, exploration, and conflict, and to be used to support nationalistic/patriotic rhetoric, often in combination with a male-orientated view of the world. New forms or opportunities for such activities – space exploration and colonization, for instance – stimulate new kinds of adventure stories. In order to be recognized as adventure stories, however, these must retain many of the traditional elements, such as a deserving hero who is tested, a journey to distant places, fights with villains/enemies/rivals, and a triumphant conclusion, usually involving a return home. Equally, when the conventions associated with a genre arise from a way of life or set of behaviours that has become less visible and influential in society, that genre will contract or even become dormant.

The religious story offers an example of a genre in decline. As the historical overview in Chapter 1 shows, the very roots of children's publishing lie in this area, but during the 20th century, as Western societies became more secular, the characters and conventions traditionally associated with religious stories – pious children, conversions, missionaries, good deaths for those who led holy lives – came to be seen as outmoded and largely disappeared. Indeed, religious stories became the subject of ridicule, and religious figures featured as stock villains for many other genres, from the pseudo clerics in John Masefield's fantasy *The Box of Delights* (1935) to the abusive figure known as 'The Prophet' in Carol Lynch Williams's *The Chosen One* (2010), a realistic story about growing up in a fundamentalist sect. As the 21st century approached, two phenomena – increasingly multicultural populations in many countries and the rise of fundamentalism – stimulated a revival of writing for children in which religion plays a central role. As the discussion of the *Left Behind* books (1998–) by Tim LaHaye and Jerry B. Jenkins in Chapter 6 shows, there are signs of new activity in this area of children's publishing. However, since many of the key features of the genre have been lost or radically changed, and most fuse plots involving religion with elements of other genres (the family story, the problem novel, the war story, the detective story, the adventure story), the renewed interest in religious writing may prove to be less about reviving a genre than developing a theme.

Much can be learned about what children's literature is telling children about how the world works from tracing the rise and fall of genres, but perhaps even more revealing is observing how individual genres retain core characteristics while adapting to changing circumstances. One of the longest established and most dynamic genres is the family story, making it a good vehicle for exploring key changes in children's literature over time. As will become clear, the story of the family as told in texts for children is an important source of information about the social, economic, and political forces which have shaped the institution of the family since commercial publishing for children began in the 18th century. More than that, the family story emerges as one of the means for adjusting and regulating understanding of what families are and how they work. To identify change, it is necessary to start by looking at the foundations and legacy of the family story.

Family fictions and...

For most children, childhood takes place in families, and families are ubiquitous in children's literature. From the vigilant middle-class paragons of parents addressed by 18th-century writers to the neglectful, uncultured, and obtuse parents in Roald Dahl's *Matilda* (1988), the vast majority of children's books reference characters' families and domestic lives to some degree. Families in the stories that make up this genre – sometimes referred to as the domestic story – do not merely provide the context, however, but are also the subject of the narratives. At one level, this makes it very easy to recognize family stories: they concentrate on the individuals who make up the central family and the relationships between them. Typically, the family in question begins as a complete, loving nuclear family with two parents and a happy, comfortable life. The story usually charts what happens when family life is disrupted by, for example, the absence or death of one or both parents, a financial crisis, or the need to make a new home in a distant place (often, the three are linked).

One of the best-known and most influential family stories, Louisa May Alcott's *Little Women* (1868), characteristically begins with Mr March away (he is ministering to troops during the American Civil War). Although the March family is middle class in education, values, and social role, their income has been sorely reduced; this, and Mr March's absence, tests the entirely female family he has left behind. The structure moves between chapters that focus on the pleasures and crises of family life, and chapters which follow individual sisters as each is forced to confront her personal temptation. Ultimately, the family is reunited – at which point, it is confirmed that the girls have become the little women their father hoped to find them. They have learned to put others before self, work before pleasure, and have internalized the Christian messages associated with *The Pilgrim's Progress*, an intertext which provides the narrative spine of the book. The March girls' growth is largely attributed to good parenting: Marmee has been on hand, observing and responding to each of her daughters' needs, while Mr March's absence and his expectations of what he will find on his return subtly enhance his authority and influence. In working to live up to his expectations, the girls treat him as the voice of their conscience – a paternal superego – and so regulate themselves. An enduring message of the family story is that distance and disturbance do not divide families, but make demands on them that can be strengthening.

The structure and pattern of *Little Women* is repeated in many family stories. The series about the Pepper family (1881–1961) by Margaret Sidney (Harriet M. Lothrop) has at its centre Mamsie, a widow mother in the Marmee mould whose hard work and strong moral character help her hold the family together and bring out the best in her 'five little Peppers'. Readers spend time with each of the young Peppers before the family's virtues are rewarded when a wealthy benefactor takes them into his home and provides for them. E. Nesbit's stories are clearly in this tradition: comfortable families fallen on hard times, dead mothers, absent fathers, and family fortunes restored. Nesbit's family stories are also typical of the genre in the way they place each child character at the centre of a particular adventure which subtly teaches a lesson in behaviour. They do, however, signal a notable change: the absence of the underlying religious message of earlier family stories. This shift is accompanied by a lessening in the importance of parents as guiding figures.

Secularization and the accompanying diminution in the authority of parents became permanent features of the family story during the 20th century. Although her father was a bishop, there is no mention of God or organized religion in the family stories Noel Streatfeild wrote between 1936 and 1968, and the parents or other caring figures in them are often unworldly and lack practical skills, meaning that the children must manage themselves and sometimes act as providers as well. It is not only artists who can be domestically vague: the brilliant scientist-parents in Madeleine L'Engle's books about the Murry family (1962, 1973) also rely on their competent children, who plant the garden, make warm drinks in the middle of the night, and rescue their parents and each other from the forces of evil the scientists' experiments have brought to light. (L'Engle's Christian faith is evident in her writing, but the Murry family are not portrayed as practising Christians.) The same is true of the Casson family in Hilary McKay's series of books (2001–7) about four children of artist-parents who live separately and are both caught up in their painting. The children live with their loving but distracted mother and largely parent each other and manage the household.

These examples suggest some ways in which the family story has responded to social and cultural changes in the nature of the family, but they do not show the extent to which the white, middle-class, nuclear family which dominated children's literature until well into the 20th century has been replaced by families that are more representative of those in society. Since the 1960s, working-class families, families from different racial and ethnic backgrounds, and families which are not headed by two parents of opposite sex have featured in family stories. The inclusion of more kinds of families did not necessarily affect the basic characteristics of the family story, however. Mildred D. Taylor's books about the Logans, a black family in the American South in the 1930s, conform closely to the genre conventions typified by *Little Women*. The family is raised by two strong, capable, respected, heterosexual parents; each of the children in the family has to deal with problems, and the family has to face a crisis together, making their bonds even closer. A variation on the conventions of the family story results from the fact that the Logan family is black and the book is concerned with the racism that affects how they live. This means that *Roll of Thunder, Hear My Cry* pays more attention to the family's interactions with the wider world than do many family stories.

There is, in fact, a thread that runs through this genre comprising families who live so far away from society that such interactions are rare, if indeed they are possible. From *The Family Robinson Crusoe* by Swiss writer Johann David Wyss (translated into English in 1814 and now generally known as *The Swiss Family Robinson*) through the stories of the Ingalls family's journey across the expanding United States as told by Laura Ingalls Wilder (1932–43), children's literature has given rise to a well-developed subgenre of stories about self-sufficient and adventurous families. Typically, the Robinsons and the Ingalls have set out to improve their circumstances, pointing to one of the less visible but most powerful factors affecting the family story: the role of the family as an economic unit.

Coinciding with the introduction of commercial children's book publishing are the rise of the bourgeois nuclear family and the dominance of capitalism, two powerful forces shaping the way families are portrayed in children's fiction (O'Malley 2003; Reynolds 2007). In our current age of rapid travel and instant communication, families can be together physically or virtually more or less on demand, but for much of its history, the family story for children has reflected a different reality. From the 18th century to the early decades of the 20th century, whether driven by the need to follow work, the economics of colonization, the exigencies of empire-building, the vagaries of politics, or the dictates of military, administrative, and religious careers, the history of the family has often been one of long separations. This may account for the insistence in family stories on family togetherness, on the one hand, and families' abilities to be strengthened by separation, on the other. Togetherness may be an